A Practical Guide for

Kindergarten Teachers

A Practical
Guide for
Kindergarten
Teachers

Mabel Evelyn Miller

PARKER PUBLISHING COMPANY, INC.
West Nyack, N.Y.

Third Printing..... June, 1971

PRINTED IN THE UNITED STATES OF AMERICA
13–690883–7   B & P

DEDICATION

I dedicate this book to all my kindergartners, from whom I learn so much. They make every day's teaching a delightful experience.

Why I Decided to Write This Book

Kindergarten teachers are constantly challenged to meet the individual needs of five-to-six-year-olds. They search for methods to effectively develop activities from children's interests and to use those interests to teach necessary skills that will prepare children for first grade. Today's classrooms are frequently overcrowded and today's children are as different as the patterns and colors of a kaleidoscope. Creative teaching is often abandoned by the over-worked kindergarten teacher, as a goal too difficult to attain without curriculum helps or teaching aids.

A Practical Guide for Kindergarten Teachers is a how-to-do-it guide, which tells its readers, "The methods presented here are experienced-based, teacher-tested and practical. You can use them in your classroom; you can pattern your own ideas after them and make them work with *your* students in *your* classroom."

Chapters of the book were written to tell teachers, "Kindergarten children behave in these specific ways; they endure these anxieties; they have these capabilities and desires for creative expression. Kindergartners need these individual attentions and personal satisfactions." The book discusses the many underlying causes for disruptive behavior in the kindergarten and suggests practical ways for solving behavioral problems.

I know how important it is for the kindergarten teacher to understand and deal wisely with individual differences, for they are particularly crucial problems in the kindergarten. A chapter discusses these individual differences in an attempt to help teachers solve the adjustment difficulties common to five-year-olds. Often school is the first place where some children meet acceptance, or find security and love. Kindergarten may also be the first place where some children meet the firm, quiet discipline which they unconsciously seek. School may be the place where a spoiled, over-privileged child first meets the need to share, or to consider the rights and desires of others.

I have presented teacher-tested ways to challenge the bright child, the slow learner, the average, the immature and the culturally deprived child. I share, with the teacher, "ways-that-work" when dealing with kindergartners who are over-aggressive or withdrawn. I have used these methods to give such children the satisfaction and joy of group acceptance and individual recognition. These ways worked for me. They will work for my readers.

My years of experience have prompted me to suggest remedies which will cure a painful case of bad parent-teacher rapport, for instance, between little Oscar's teacher and his mother. The little Oscar his mother adores just *isn't* always the same little Oscar who is annoying his teacher every minute of every hour!

In writing this book I had these basic objectives which I want to share with other kindergarten teachers, the same objectives I have had in all my years of kindergarten teaching:

1. *To present material that will help all children, on every learning level, to be intensely aware of their world and the ways their reaction to each part of it affects the things they want to learn.*

2. *To present ways which will help children to acquire new knowledge of their world and to use this knowledge in their daily lives as enriching and satisfying experiences.*

Creative teaching, using creative methods and materials, is the only way to attain such objectives. In this book I have presented ways in which the constant "play" that is so integral a part of the good kindergarten can become challenging activities with great learning potentials, for all children, on any level of comprehension. Throughout the book I have shown how creative methods can develop a child's basic skills and native abilities, how they can encourage his creative ideas and stimulate him to question, investigate and experiment.

I have used classroom case histories and anecdotes to help teachers to relate ideas, theories, suggestions and materials to their own interests and concerns, applicable to their own situations. This book shares my experiences, methods and practices, which have been successfully used to challenge the kindergartners' many areas of interest.

The book also includes ways which have been used to successfully teach the physically or mentally handicapped child, or the emotionally disturbed, in the regular classroom. Every kindergarten teacher, at some point in her career, is likely to be faced with the necessity to teach such a child. Often the teacher can play an important role in making the life of such a child happier and can help him to find acceptance in his group.

There are chapters which offer units of study, or suggestions for units of study, which are developed from children's varied interests. These ideas are both practical and workable, and are based on the sound theory that *a child's learning about a subject area is commensurate with the degree of his personal involvement in that subject*. These units employ projects, techniques and subject materials which will appeal to a child's senses, to his curiosity and to his need for personal participation in a room project.

Games that teach skills are suggested in every subject area. Various experience-based and teacher-tested techniques are presented throughout the book. Problems and their solutions are discussed. In this book I have shared my ideas and methods, both general and specific, because they have proved that they will work for me. They will also work for *you*.

MABEL EVELYN MILLER

ACKNOWLEDGMENTS

I wish to express deep appreciation to these people whose support, suggestions and cooperation have helped me in the writing of this book:

Ara K. Smith, Superintendent of Michigan City Area Schools, and a loyal friend.

Alma Koza, Assistant Superintendent of Elementary Education (recently deceased).

Ray Steele, my principal at Long Beach School, a friend and educator, whose never-failing encouragement and assistance helped me in developing teaching ideas and projects.

James Wagner and Kenneth Humbert, Graphics Department, McIntire Media Center, Michigan City Area Schools, to whom I am indebted for the pictures in this book.

Marie Wolff, Art teacher, Laporte, Indiana, whose faith in me helped to make this book possible.

Florence Coffin, principal, Marsh School, who graciously offered her time to listen, help and advise.

Ruth Millbranth, teacher and dear friend, whose sincere interest, encouragement and sound advice are so deeply appreciated.

Anne Sierk, fellow researcher and friend, with whom I discussed many ideas and projects.

Fellow teachers, who have been so cooperative.

Parents of my kindergartners, dear friends who never once failed to give me their loyal support and confidence.

The editors of *Instructor* Magazine, who so graciously allowed me to use material from my previously published articles.

McGraw-Hill Book Company and Willis Music Company, for permission to use song titles or words of songs.

Finally, I thank the members of my family: Delbert, my husband, for the many patiently borne inconveniences the writing of this book has caused him; my daughter and her family; my sister and brother, all of whom have encouraged me in my work.

10

Contents

11

4227

1

How to Be
an Effective Teacher
in an
Overcrowded Classroom

Most educators agree that the kindergarten can offer more effective learning situations when the enrollment is kept at a maximum of twenty-five children. In these modern days of population explosion, inadequate school facilities and teacher scarcity, it is a rare kindergarten that has such a small enrollment. Kindergarten teachers are confronted with thirty-five to fifty children in rooms that were meant to comfortably accommodate twenty. Quite often the equipment is so inadequate that a teacher must have courage, creativeness, great patience and ingenuity to meet all the problems that will result from a large enrollment.

Positive Attitude Toward Problem

The kindergarten teacher must always approach any problem in a positive way if she wants to offer opportunities for maximum learning in an overcrowded classroom.

The mental attitude of a teacher at any time is important, but it is doubly vital when her teaching conditions are far from ideal. She must feel a deep sense of personal self-confidence and dignity. She should be able to accept the less desirable characteristics of children as well as their good qualities.

She should:

1. Really love and enjoy her kindergartners. She should let them *feel* her affection by making encouraging remarks about their activities; by putting a comforting arm around little shoulders; by giving children some special, much needed attention.

2. Show genuine warmth toward each individual child, however difficult the child may be at times.

3. Smile and laugh often. Share amusing situations with her students. Never be too busy or preoccupied to be excited over a bug, a tooth that is loose, the acquisition of a new pet, or a pending visit from grandparents.

4. Have enthusiasm for new projects the children suggest and a vast store of creative and exciting ideas, and offer to help when they need her direction.

5. Provide a program of varied activities suited to the individual needs of each group of children she teaches.

6. Be alerted to the individual interests of her kindergartners, the TV programs that are especially valuable, their home concerns, their individual trips or projects.

7. Allow kindergartners to satisfy curiosity, investigate, experiment, handle, examine, and talk about objects. If a child becomes destructive, the teacher should find out if he is satisfying his curiosity or is releasing tensions, so she may wisely help him with his problem.

8. Try to see good in each child and to be fair and wise in making judgments when controversies or conflicts in personality arise.

9. Show a child, by her continued love for him, that he is forgiven for misdemeanors, and remains a valued member of his group.

10. Guide children, carefully and wisely, when setting up behavior and safety controls, and let them share in setting up reasonable boundaries and limits.
11. Respect individual differences, allow for varying levels of achievement among children, and eliminate any feeling of competition among kindergartners.
12. Allow each child to succeed in some areas, before their classmates.
13. Learn to gain the confidence of the quiet, shy or withdrawn children, and help the aggressive, too ebullient child to adjust his behavior to the group.
14. Provide ways in which kindergartners may make choices for themselves, but help them to sometimes sublimate their own feelings and desires to help make choices that are best for the group.
15. Always use praise and a positive approach to those things a child can do *right* and *well,* even if he presents a severe discipline problem. Young children react to praise when scolding or disapproval goes unheeded.
16. Use a clear voice in the crowded classroom, one that will require careful listening on the part of every child.
17. *Never* allow children to laugh at each other's mistakes or misfortunes.
18. Avoid threats.
19. Never make promises unless she is positive she can fulfill them.
20. Govern children, when possible, by lifted eyebrows, a warning glance, a gentle but restraining remark or touch.
21. Never make an entire class suffer for the misdeeds of a few individuals.

The kindergarten teacher who serenely accepts her crowded classroom, whatever its over-populated and under-equipped state, will devise many ways of meeting her teaching problems and will regard them as a challenge to her ingenuity. As she guides her kindergartners to "learning by doing" she will find new resourcefulness within herself to meet whatever demands are made on her time and energy in her overcrowded classroom.

Organization of Classroom Activities

Organization of activities, equipment, and materials, is the key to successful teaching in an overcrowded classroom. The teacher should give much thought to the arrangement of furniture and equipment in the room, so that she and the children can move about with a minimum of effort but a maximum enjoyment of facilities.

There should be regular daily routines, which the children can help to establish, activities which they like and understand, and in which they regularly participate. Young children want to know what they can expect of their kindergarten room and of their teacher, and what she expects of them. They need the security of sameness in many daily routines, but they also need the challenge of constantly changing activities. The wise teacher will find that delicate balance between these diverse needs and set up room situations that offer the beloved security of the known with the exciting anticipation of the new and unknown.

On those occasions when the kindergarten teacher must be absent for a day or longer, her plans should be so intricately detailed that a substitute teacher can proceed with the usual routines exactly in the usual manner. This careful planning will help kindergartners to behave in a normal manner and will facilitate the regular teacher's return to a room that has run smoothly, without incident, in her absence.

All books and materials should have their own places, where children can easily reach them, and return them. Attractive folders, for loose activity papers of all kinds, can be made from bright 12″ x 18″ construction paper and kept neatly stacked, with each child's name written on his folder in large print. The child takes pride in recognizing his own name, in making a creative picture on his folder, and in the possession of an object which belongs exclusively to him. Such folders, when filled with a child's work, are objects which he is happy to take home for parent inspection and approval.

Records and reports can be done by the teacher with a minimum of effort when she has carefully and efficiently planned her work. When possible the kindergarten teacher will want to delegate easy-to-do tasks to her children. They not only are delighted to perform such tasks, but the responsibility helps them to gain self-respect, confidence in their own ability and a mature sense of obligation to the group. When children learn to carry on routine tasks calmly and without excitement even in the face of an emergency (and emergencies *often* occur when there are thirty to fifty children in a room), it helps the teacher to have extra time for more exacting activities.

Leaders can be appointed on a day-to-day or weekly basis, and these children take attendance, pass out and gather up books, papers, folders, art supplies, give out milk and cookies, run errands to the principal's office, and organize games. The more responsibility a young child is given, the more he is capable of handling with efficiency. Even the most immature and irresponsible child in the room will proudly do the tasks required of him when he is a leader. What he lacks in skill he will compensate for in enthusiasm.

Young children, in order to receive the most benefit from their learning program, need to help in its planning whenever possible. In kindergarten, more than other grades, learning can be integrated with the children's interests or should directly evolve from those interests, and the opportunities for learning are limitless. Children take great interest and pride in a project when it is *theirs*.

The kindergarten room should display these interests, the pictures children have made, the things about which they are curious, the answers they have found to their questions. A room's display areas should never be dominated by seasonal or holiday displays, but should be chiefly used for their continuing interests.

Most kindergartners can't read, of course, but they become very curious about those symbols that represent words and the names of things. Large, brightly colored letters on display areas intrigue their interests and bring out questions and exchanges of opinions.

"AREN'T YOU GLAD . . . ?" or "WE LEARN ABOUT . . ." catch their attention. "WHAT DO YOU THINK WILL HAPPEN?" "TRAINS BRING US . . ." "WE WANT TO

KNOW THESE THINGS . . ." and "THINGS WE LIKE TO DO" are only a few challenging titles for displays, which will stimulate the interest of children. They talk about what the words say, they find letters there that are in their own names, they often will busily copy the letters on paper when they have free activity time.

Some kindergartners can quite accurately use scissors at the beginning of school, others acquire the skill by mid-year. These children can help their teacher in many ways, while less proficient children find the satisfaction of achievement at less exacting small tasks.

The well-organized, efficient kindergarten teacher employs many teaching aids for the individual learning needs of her groups. She will want to make many of these herself, using materials that are bright and attractive. If she enlists the aid of her kindergartners in collecting some of these materials or in bringing them from home, the children will be doubly interested in their use. Details for the preparation of teaching aids will be given in later chapters of this book.

Continuously Challenged, Happy Children Are Easier to Control

Good discipline is important in any classroom, but in the overcrowded kindergarten room it is absolutely essential. How can the teacher, from the beginning of school, consistently maintain good discipline in a room full of young children who must learn to live and work with each other in an unfamiliar environment? Keep them busy! A busy, interested child is a happy child. In school it is his teacher's responsibility to provide continuous and challenging activities which will start him on his long, fascinating search for the things he wants most to know.

The teacher's task of keeping a roomful of squirming, noisy children happily busy may seem impossible, but it can be done. Planning and organization again are the essential requisites for a continuously challenging kindergarten program. In the early part of the school year activities must change frequently, so that the child with the shortest attention span will not find time to distract his classmates by sounds, antics or physical aggression.

Relaxing activities of all kinds should be used now and throughout the kindergarten year. Suggested games that teach and relax are found in another chapter of this book. Quick, quiet exercises that teach left, right, in, out, up, down, can be used; rhythms are excellent as relaxers. Gay songs that require bodily movements, role-playing, and purposeful dramatizations all serve to relax a child's tensions while they challenge his active mind. Fingerplays that are intricate enough to require every child's concentration are fun for him, get his immediate attention and sustain it for a short time.

If a kindergarten teacher wants to be assured of good discipline in her room she will always *plan more activities for the day than she can possibly do.* She may find it expedient to postpone one activity and organize another to meet with children's interests. When the active, mischievous boy bounces into her room in the morning and demands, "What are we going to do exciting *today?*" he knows that his teacher has a *lot* of ideas, a lot of plans to keep him and all the other little squirmers like him so busy they won't have time to get into trouble. Moving smoothly from one activity to another, so that the children do not realize they are being cleverly maneuvered into good behavior, makes a rigorous schedule for the teacher, but it repays all the efforts she puts into its planning and execution. When she says goodby to her charges at the end of a kindergarten session she knows that not once has she had a really troublesome incident of bad behavior.

Planning for constant activity does not mean that a teacher must strictly adhere to her full program, nor be concerned if she fails to accomplish all that she planned, to cover all the material she meant to cover in one period. She must be flexible enough to give young children time to look at and examine objects, to experiment, to touch, taste, lift, manipulate, to plunge into activities with excitement, or to dawdle and dream. Her day's program is a full but flexible one, allowing time for free activity choices; a program adaptable enough to allow much time for interesting discussion and learning about some unexpected happening. There are many exciting and totally unplanned events in the kindergartner's daily life and the teacher must always be ready to see their potentials for good learning and capitalize on them.

Children May Help Set Standards of Behavior

In making preparations for the beginning of school, the kindergarten teacher whose room is overcrowded can do many things which will make living together in cramped quarters easier for her and the children. Perhaps it will be impossible to have the name of *every* boy and girl who will appear on that first day, but she can become familiar with those names which she does have, print them in large, clear letters and display them in the room. On that first day of school she can point out his or her name to each child, and explain that she was *waiting* and looking forward to having that individual in her room. Learning names quickly is very important to the young child, for he is completely self-centered at this point in his development, and his being one of a very large group of children can sometimes be very frightening. It gives the five-year-old a real feeling of security to know that his new teacher *knows him,* and his name is *right there!* He may not recognize his own name, but she told him it was there and already he trusts her. They like each other. There may be forty-nine other children in the room, but his teacher knows *him!*

Not all young children can, at first, understand the inevitable noise that accompanies the presence of thirty to fifty children in a room. Coming from a quiet home to a noisy schoolroom full of active children can be very disturbing to the child who is accustomed to playing alone. The understanding teacher will provide some spot in the room where quiet, timid children can sometimes retreat and make sure that they are not annoyed by others who want to tease and disturb.

Kindergarten presents a wonderful opportunity for all children to learn about living with their contemporaries. In the overcrowded classroom there are certain rules of courtesy that must be observed when many people live together for hours. The teacher can discuss these rules with her kindergartners, and guide them while they decide on rules and standards of conduct and acceptable behavior. When someone forgets the rules, they can all decide, when the early planning is done, what privileges must be given up, until the child can remember the rules. *Children who push or cut in line must go to the end of the line.* Everybody will agree that this rule is fair. *A child who cannot work or play well in a group should be asked to find another activity.* This rule, too, the children are agreed upon. When children help to decide rules for acceptable behavior, they are more inclined to abide by, without rebellion, the denial of an abused privilege.

Some playground rules are forbidden for children of all ages, such as standing up in a swing, and must be obeyed for this reason. Such a rule makes sense to young children when they are convinced "big kids" must abide by it, too.

The discerning teacher will be aware of tensions that build up in her room between conflicting personalities. She can take measures to ease them by changing activity-table areas, by unobtrusively arranging for different associations and friendships to develop.

Young children can be quietly and subtly drawn into many activities that are of real help to the teacher of the overcrowded room. Praise does far more to enlist eager help than any demand she might make. "I saw Mary carefully putting her finished puzzle away. She may choose a helper to finish the other puzzles." "John takes care of the toys he uses and puts them back in their own box on the shelf. He may straighten all the toys on the shelf." "Jimmy is such a good helper in the room. His eyes see many things that he can do." Even the laziest, most irresponsible child in the room can't resist sweet-talk like that and will work so hard a mother wouldn't recognize her child!

The wise teacher gives responsibility only when a child shows he is capable of assuming it; but she encourages other children to accept responsibility by a remark, "Lisa, you did your work very well. You may help Charles and Betty." "That was good thinking, Ricky. You knew where to find the materials we needed."

Good discipline can rarely be maintained in a room when quick-thinking, quick-acting children are required to wait on slow workers. Unoccupied, lively children tend to get into trouble. Some kindergartners are awkward and unskilled in the use of their small hand muscles and even the simplest activity with crayons and scissors takes them a long time. These children need to have opportunity to work without any feeling of pressure, but often they will welcome help and encouragement from those children who have already finished their activity. Such offered and accepted help benefits both children, and the slow worker, because he is praised, gains much-needed self-confidence.

By helping to formulate rules for acceptable behavior, young children learn that each child's opinion is considered, that each child must "take turns" in all activities, whether it means standing in line for the slide or holding up a hand for permission to talk. Children dislike being interrupted, or not being listened to when they are telling an exciting story; but it comes to some of them as a surprise that their teacher likes to have them listen to *her* without their interruptions. Observing rules of courtesy makes life in the overcrowded classroom much easier for all its occupants. Children soon realize that their teacher and companions expect acceptable behavior from them and they know the others will be quick to correct them when they disobey the rules they have helped to make.

The teacher can devise many quiet games to help children achieve acceptable behavior. She can close her eyes while they pick up toys or chairs and tiptoe to the table; or ask them to walk on quiet feet, "mice feet," or to play an Indian who "walks through the forest without breaking a twig." She may merely turn her back, while she allows some rowdy, boisterous children to compose themselves and restore order (amid much audible rustling and whispering). A suggestion such as "I love to see your eyes when I talk to you," or "when I read a story to you," proves an effective attention sustainer. "How nice you look when your feet are on the floor, and your hands are in your lap," helps to keep roving hands from annoying one's neighbors. "How quiet you were when you came up here for the story. You were so quiet I could hear the clock ticking," encourages more silence. When children are especially restless their teacher can intrigue and quiet them by playing a "whispering" game, where all directions are given in whispers.

At the end of a particularly trying day one teacher admonishes her kindergartners to "leave those noisy boys and girls at home tomorrow. Make those talkers stay right in bed *all* day. Bring the quiet child to school with you." There are giggles and much appreciation of the humor. The next day she asks, "Did you leave your noisy selves at home in bed?" Of course everyone did, and every child *is* much quieter because he is playing a role.

There is one suggestion the kindergarten teacher would never make, however, if she wanted momentary peace and tranquility. At the mere mention of the word "flying," a roomful of lively children can take off, airborne, with accompanying noises that are deafening!

Learning in the Overcrowded Classroom

The kindergarten teacher in the overcrowded classroom does not have an easy task. She will often be exhausted, frustrated and baffled by the problems that confront her as she tries to meet the needs of the children in her room. They have entered kindergarten with varying degrees of preschool learning, emotional endowment and environmental background. Many have, from birth, been deprived of all but the barest necessities, a few may speak only a foreign language and know nothing of the customs and ways of their companions. Young children are often bewildered when they come from homes where they have been the center of attention and where the adults in their lives devote much time to them, and find they must suddenly compete with many children for the attention of one adult, their teacher. The unavoidable noise caused by the presence of many children living and playing in the room is more than some of them can tolerate. In the first weeks of school the kindergarten teacher often has to live through many crises, settle many arguments, be wise, loving and patient as she meets all the demands made upon her physical and mental health.

Her attitude toward her task is a positive one of enthusiasm, anticipation and acceptance. She is ready to offer her children humor, understanding, compassion and love; to her job she brings creativeness, ingenuity and the capacity for long hours and hard work. She will provide her kindergartners with the time to question, experiment, try out new ideas, participate in new activities and explore unknown areas of learning. Her carefully planned program will enable every child to have the opportunity to acquire new skills and enjoy experiences that will result in creative thinking.

When children's eager minds, their intense curiosity and their desire to learn are combined with the kindergarten teacher's ability to meet those endless needs, maximum learning must inevitably result—even in the overcrowded classroom.

BIBLIOGRAPHY

Brogan, Peggy, and Lorene K. Fox, *Helping Children Learn.* Yonkers-on-Hudson, N.Y.: World Book Company, 1955.

Gesell, Arnold, and Frances L. Ilg, *The Child from Five to Ten.* New York: Harper and Bros., Publishers, 1946.

Jenkins, Gladys Gardner, *Helping Children Reach Their Potential.* Chicago: Scott Foresman and Company, 1961.

Lambert, Hazel M., *Teaching the Kindergarten Child.* New York: Harcourt, Brace and Co., Inc., 1958.

Symonds, Percival M., "Personality of the Teacher," *Journal of Education Research,* XL (May, 1947), pp. 652–71.

Wills, Clarice, and Lucille Lindborg, *Kindergarten for Today's Children.* Chicago: Follett Publishing Company, 1967.

Wills, Clarice Dechent, and William H. Stegeman, *Living in the Kindergarten.* Chicago: Follett Publishing Company, 1956.

2

Ways to Help
Kindergartners Achieve
Self-discipline
and Good Citizenship

Most young children begin their lives in kindergarten with open minds, intense curiosity, few prejudices and a huge capacity to absorb new ideas. In their first year of school, kindergartners are helped to discover all the countless ways in which they may acquire new knowledge, and reinforce and enlarge upon old knowledge. They need direction in learning how to live and function happily and usefully in a group. They begin to understand why the rights and needs of other children make it necessary to establish rules of acceptable behavior in the room. Their early training, preschool experiences and kindergarten learning make an excellent basis upon which character can be built.

The kindergarten teacher has the privilege, as well as the grave responsibility, of guiding her young students to make wise decisions, to acquire good habits of behavior, to learn consideration of the rights of others and to accept possible defeats and disappointments which may result from their inexperience in choice-making.

4227

Young children need freedom of thought and movement to help them direct their own learning activities and develop their own standards of acceptable behavior, and they require that self-discipline which will serve as a valuable framework upon which to build character. Even in today's society, with its modern learning theories and techniques, it often requires courage on the part of a kindergarten teacher to allow her children these freedoms. In our democracy the freedom to express oneself is an inviolable right—unless it occurs in the classroom and disrupts the absolute quiet which some teachers and educators still regard as the atmosphere most conducive to learning.

When children are encouraged to actively participate in their own government, to help plan their own activities, to express opinions which may result in lengthy discussions, inevitably there will be a disruption of what was once called "good discipline"; but the learning which results from such group planning and communication is immeasurable. The child whose opinion has never been valued at home may find that what he has to contribute in his room is important to the group. The boy who has never had the courage to speak out alone may be brave enough to cast his verbal observations into the shared conversation and so gain confidence in expressing himself. The girl who loudly asks for attention may learn her first lesson in humility when she becomes aware that she is now part of a group and that all voices are heard, all opinions are considered.

The teacher who wisely allows her kindergartners the time to plan, and guides them as they strive toward group organization of activities, must also be prepared to show proof of the learning which results from such planning. She may be challenged by parents or educators to defend her methods.

Her contention that she is allowing her kindergartners to develop self-discipline is valid. She may be asked, "What is meant by self-discipline?" The term is not listed by some dictionaries. One defines self-discipline as the "correction or regulation of oneself for the sake of improvement."

For the purposes of this book, in suggesting ways to help kindergartners to achieve self-discipline, the term may be defined as "training the self in behaviors that are acceptable to other mem-

bers of one's group," or "the readiness of an individual to sublimate the needs of self to the needs of the group." The kindergartner who learns to control his own feelings and desires, to consider
the rights of others, to be responsible for his own behavior, has
acquired the basis for a strong character and the background for
unlimited freedom to learn.

Positive Approach to Good Discipline Most Effective

The kindergarten teacher's role in helping the child to acquire
self-discipline is a vital one. She must truly believe in the child,
so that he can believe in himself. She will need to find frequent
ways to show him that she has faith in his *ability* to establish his
own controls, and she must guide him wisely as he experiments
with these new ideas and concepts of self-discipline. This guidance, so necessary to the child's development, must be subtle
enough to convince him that *he* helped to make some decisions;
he can be responsible for his own actions; *he* had a voice in making the rules in his room.

There are many times during the kindergarten day when a
teacher must use judicious restraint to keep the room atmosphere
most conducive to good learning. The wise teacher will find ingenious ways to get her desired results, rather than scolding or
laying down harsh, adult ultimatums. She can assure the children
once again that she knows they are "grown-up" enough and "old"
enough to make their own decisions about behavior, and to this
they will agree, wholeheartedly. She may suggest an effective
plan to "leave the naughty kindergartner that came to school with
you at home tomorrow. He (or she) disturbs the other children
here. Bring that nice kindergartner to school, the one who knows
how to play well with other children." Disruptive children often
will respond to this game, and their behavior the following day
generally improves. The game is fun and more acceptable behavior from the whole group invariably results from the teacher's
method of control.

She uses praise whenever possible and encourages her children
to *think* about the reasons for unpleasantness in their room.
She encourages them to talk freely about their own mistakes in

sharing and in fair play. They are given time to discuss and consider all suggestions that are made. The teacher may need to be adroit in terminating such a discussion, before the children who are still too immature for decision-making become restless and begin to disturb others.

Kindergartners quickly learn that their acceptable behavior and pleasant work together makes all school experiences more fun. As a group they can have more privileges. When they can be depended upon to cooperate they can do more exciting things and take more field trips. Learning consideration for others is an important step in growth of character and citizenship.

While helping her kindergartners to learn self-control, the teacher refrains from coercion; instead she sets up many situations which will help the children to make decisions that are satisfying to them. Young children staunchly defend and champion those rules of behavior which they have helped to establish. Rebellion against those rules, by the few, is frowned upon by the group. Kindergartners are often indignant when older children, deliberately or unwittingly, disobey their safety rules for hall or playground.

Faith of Teacher in Students

The kindergarten teacher must have faith in her children, from all ethnic and cultural groups. She must show a warm, genuine acceptance of them to receive their maximum cooperation. Young children are surprisingly perceptive and they demand proof that the adults in their world are honest and trustworthy. A few words of praise for the immature child who is trying to zip his coat will keep him patiently practicing until he can do the task. When a child has had no previous opportunity to exercise self-control, he needs much praise as he struggles to control his temper. The child who has known little kindness or consideration from others must have his teacher's patient help in overcoming his distrust.

A teacher's faith in the slow learner or the physically handicapped child makes him more acceptable to his classmates. Her praise for the achievements of these children prompts the group to encourage their slow progress. She must be careful that a child is never embarrassed by her remarks, and she will welcome whatever contribution they can make to the room activity.

The child who is aggressive and always unkind to his classmates desperately needs her love and faith. A little boy, Jonathan, was reminded by his teacher, "I *know* you really want to stop fighting with other boys on the playground. You had such good ideas that day we decided that fighting with other children makes everyone unhappy."

"But my dad says I gotta fight when kids push me around," Jonathan protested.

"Your father and I both know you are big enough to decide when children are just playing rough games and when they mean to hurt you. Jonathan, I trust you not to fight with the boys in your room. I *know* you are going to be a good friend to everyone here." The teacher of a boy like Jonathan may need to remind him every day that she believes in him, but her constant faith helps him to believe in himself. Acceptable behavior becomes a desirable goal, although not an immediate one, for aggressive Jonathan to achieve. It is a goal he will strive to reach, because somebody knows he can. His teacher has to be patient as Jonathan struggles for self-discipline, but if he succeeds in curbing his temper, they both will have a warm feeling of success in his shared struggle toward adjusting to his group.

Angie was a child from a large family whose children were frequently in trouble at school and in their neighborhood. From her first day in kindergarten she was a trial to her teacher and her classmates. Her miserable home life had taught her that lying and deception were means by which she could provide herself with things she so desperately wanted. At five Angie felt she had a right to take anything if nobody caught her taking it. She used deception and belligerence to get her own way. Her classmates resisted her at first and were outraged at her actions. Then they began to ignore and reject her which made her behavior more intolerable than ever.

Her teacher soon understood that Angie was not only intelligent but full of inner conflict. Much of what she did was for personal satisfaction, but she desperately wanted attention. She needed to be loved, to be respected, to be a "somebody," and

Angie, in the only way she knew, was begging to learn, to be helped. Her rehabilitation was slow but effective, for she had many cultural and environmental obstacles to overcome in her struggle to be a good citizen.

One day Angie made a great show of spitting out bubble gum when she arrived at school, but sometime later she boldly blew a few large bubbles to scandalize her classmates, and smirked when they reported her behavior. Her teacher put an arm around the thin, dirty child and said, "Angie, inside of you there's a sweet little girl. Would you let her out sometime? You're the only one who can show her to me."

"Why you think that? I'm mean, and I always been mean. Ain't no sweet girl inside of *me!*"

Her teacher lifted the little chin and looked into Angie's eyes. "Don't you try to kid me," she chided gently. "There's a sweet little girl inside you and you're scared to let her out. You're scared to show us what a little lady you really *can* be."

"Ain't nobody call me sweet in my whole life. How you think I be a lady?"

"First you can spit out that gum," her teacher laughed. "Ladies in this school don't chew gum. We decided that, remember? Then you can go do something nice in the room to surprise us. And Angie," she added, as the child's eyes began to sparkle, "you can take that jump-rope out of your pocket and put it back where it belongs. Nice little ladies like you never take things that don't belong to them."

Angie learned slowly that the ways of truth, honesty and reliability were pleasant ways, and that she could be an accepted member of her group. Belief in oneself doesn't always come easily when you're five, but it helps if somebody trusts you and always expects you to do your best. Learning is easier when the rewards are trust, acceptance, approval and love.

Teacher-directed Freedom of Movement Vitally Important

Young children need to develop skill in critical thinking, so they may learn to make choices and judgments. They must learn to value freedom of activity and to use such freedom wisely. They need to make decisions and to accept responsibility, on their own level of maturity. If these choices and decisions sometimes result in unpleasant or unexpected experiences, the children need not always be protected from such results, but should be helped to understand that mistakes can and often do happen.

They must be given time to think about and discuss activities and projects. These may involve a few or all members of their group. Those children who think clearly and arrive at judgments quickly tend to be leaders among their classmates. Slower, shyer, or more immature children, who are less outgoing, must be given *much* time to decide on choices so their thinking will not be influenced by the leaders. These immature children may be reluctant to make decisions, or frightened by the need to assume responsibility for their own actions. Progress in choice-making is slow and it may take them a long time to enjoy being a part of group planning.

Helping children to self-direction is a difficult task for some teachers. They think that it consumes too much time. They prefer to make all the decisions themselves, then "condition" the children to accept them as their own. Absolute conformity to rigid rules is the goal of these teachers and they pride themselves on how well-behaved their kindergartners are, how consistently they respond to familiar situations. They would not agree that "learning by doing," in making choices for themselves, is vital to the building of character and that the children who are denied the right to help plan their own activities are not being helped to develop creative thinking and self-discipline.

It is true that some degree of conformity in school, home and public life makes living and working together easier; however, young children should be allowed to find out for themselves *why* it is best to conform in some ways. They should share in making some of the rules for living together in the classroom. The wise teacher will provide experiences that are both successful and unsuccessful, so they may realize a responsibility for their own behavior. She will guide them in identifying their own individual problems and those that are peculiar to the group, thus helping them to do critical thinking in finding solutions for these problems.

When a new activity is introduced, a few ways and means of procedure need to be presented, but children may soon be allowed to resort to their own ideas, to depend on their own initiative. The child who constantly wants to be told what to do, who needs to be instructed in every step of an activity, has failed to learn self-direction and must be helped to the realization that making one's own decisions is rewarding and leads to many new and satisfying experiences.

Children need to find out for themselves that dawdling about such routine tasks as putting away toys will deprive them of time they want to use for other, pleasant experiences. They may be introduced to timing themselves by the clock, a simple, effective learning experience that is challenging to most children. "Can you be finished when the big hand is here and the small hand is here?" Discussions about the clock bring a realization to kindergartners that they have only a certain amount of time at school each day and they must use it for many activities. They enjoy feeling that they have a part in determining how their time is spent. When they can see that using *less* time for one routine task (putting toys away) allows *more* time for a beloved game, children have learned an important lesson in comparative values.

Young children respond well to teacher-pupil planning, to helping formulate plans which directly affect them. Sometimes mistakes are made and they should help to correct these mistakes. If a group of children decides to omit rest time to allow for some special activity and as a result many children become tired and irritable, then their decision must be re-evaluated. The desires of the vigorous children must be sublimated to the needs of the easily fatigued ones, and the resulting group decision is a growth in social relationship.

When guiding children to achieve self-direction and self-discipline the teacher must always maintain a careful balance between their freedom to make choices and decisions and meaningless confusion. Young children do not like confusion in a classroom. They do not learn well in an atmosphere of noise and continuous activity. They want a certain amount of regular routine and some familiar pattern for daily activities.

Children-planned Activities

Helping kindergarten children to achieve self-discipline, to be good citizens who are valuable members of their group, is a challenging task. The alert and ingenious teacher will use children's interests to develop activities which challenge their minds and stimulate them to creative thinking. These activities should be children-planned to the limit of their abilities.

Other chapters in this book will offer children-planned activities in great detail, and many of them are projects which teach citizenship and self-discipline.

The following list covers many areas of children's interests in becoming good citizens:

1. Learning about flags.
   a. National and state flags.
   b. Where flags are displayed.
   c. When flags are displayed.
   d. Why are flags sometimes flown at half mast?
   e. Why does our flag have a certain number of stars and stripes?
   f. What did our country's first flag look like?
   g. Why did it have thirteen stripes and thirteen stars? Display early flag if possible. (In some kindergarten groups there will be much curiosity about the early states, and an exciting study of colonization, with its interesting and contrasting way of life, can be made. Their teacher will help the children to develop the areas of interest that intrigue them most.)

2. Study of map of the United States, started by children's interest in those states where many of them lived before moving to their present home.
   a. Why was the eastern side of the United States settled long before the western side?
   b. Why did our ancestors have a hard time when they traveled west? (These studies have unlimited factual material, new vocabulary words and valuable concepts

of good citizenship to offer the kindergartners, whatever their level of maturity.)

3. We are citizens of the United States. What does a grown-up citizen do to help run the government?
   a. How do people vote?
   b. A trip to see a voting machine, if possible.
   c. The experience of actually voting, by secret ballot, for the person of their choice, to be conducted in the classroom.

4. A good citizen is proud of the community in which he lives.
   a. Obeying laws.
   b. Helping to keep the community clean and pleasant. (*Litterbug* and *Clutterbug* projects are excellent ones to develop here.)

5. Truthfulness and Fairness in the schoolroom.
   a. Taking turns.
   b. Sharing.
   c. Returning articles to their owners.
   d. Asking permission to pick flowers, to cross property, etc.
   e. Keeping promises.
   f. Making sure that *all* children have the same rights.
   g. Why children are happier when they obey accepted rules.

6. Working with a purpose.
   a. What do we want to know?
   b. All the ways we know to get information, to find out about things; asking questions, looking for pictures, taking walks, watching film strips, listening to stories, hearing talks by people who know a lot about the subject, doing experiments, making things, going on field trips.

7. What do the signs say?
   a. Traffic signs.
   b. Safety signs.
   c. Signs in the classroom, in halls, etc.

8. Study of Americans who have many colors of skins, who make their livings in many ways, who live in many kinds of houses, etc. (This study may be prompted by interest in Indians, the first Americans.)

9. A good citizen observes safety rules. (This is an interesting study and almost limitless in its variety and appeal to children. Can include study of fire drills, fire, playing with matches, safety at home, at school, on the streets, in cars, on trains, etc.)

10. Leadership and Followership.
    a. Willingness to work.
    b. Self-control.
    c. Cooperative effort.
    d. Helping others.
    e. Dependability.
    f. Responsibility.
    g. Initiative, creative thinking, good ideas and how to use them. (All sorts of learning games can be developed and learning devices can be used while this area of interest is studied.)

11. Creative self-expression. (The ability to "make-do" is very important to the child's development as a good citizen.)

12. Self-reliance and self concept. (This area of interest can be an individual one. Each child can work at his own speed, in his own way. Teachers can help children learn how much they can do alone, without asking for help, and help them to find satisfaction, whatever their level of achievement.)

13. Courtesy and Helpfulness.
    a. Punctuality (Good attendance).
    b. Politeness.
    c. Helping others.
    d. Courteous words and actions.

14. Appreciation for individual skills and accomplishments.
    a. Caretaker of schoolroom. (How children can make his task easier by picking up toys, paper, etc.)

> b. Bus driver. (How children can avoid making trouble on the bus.)
>
> c. Parents.
>
> d. Brothers and sisters.
>
> e. Neighbors and others.

All of the topics above have been used successfully as children-planned activities in the classroom, and learning aids of all kinds have been employed, many of them made by the kindergartners. Language arts, vocabulary-building, new math concepts, history, geography, science, nature, art, music all become an integral part of learning to be good citizens.

Examples of Positive Methods Used to Encourage Child's Self-discipline

As a group kindergarten children can be very understanding of the problems of others. In one kindergarten, before a severely handicapped child became a member of the class, their teacher explained the child's difficulty and enlisted their aid and cooperation in his care. This meant that they would have to exert much self-control at times, for there were certain things they would not be able to do in the child's presence, for the sake of his safety. They would need to be very helpful, considerate, and self-sacrificing in some instances. All this was asked of children who had been in kindergarten only a few days, some of them not yet five years of age. Without exception, for an entire school year, the young children conducted themselves toward their less fortunate classmate with kindness, gentle restraint and consideration, showing an amazingly mature understanding of the child's problems and needs.

One little girl confided to her teacher, "I was afraid at first. I never saw anybody before who didn't grow in the regular way. Now I know people are different, just like kittens are different."

In some schools, where children of migrant workers enter and withdraw constantly, prejudices exist against them. Kindergarten is an excellent place to teach consideration and tolerance for a child's cultural background, its nationality, its race, religion, social class, its father's occupation, its heritage of family practices and beliefs, its personal conflicts, aggressions, its positive and negative values. In one kindergarten, where two new students were unable to speak English, the teacher quickly enlisted the aid of an adult citizen in the town who could interpret for them. The new pupils were invited to bring in objects which they treasured, and the visiting adult returned again to talk about the children's treasures, and their former way of life. He taught the kindergartners a few words of their new classmates' language and they sampled some of their foreign foods. It was a delightful and rewarding experience for them all, and helped them to accept one another more easily, to understand that there are good things in every culture.

When one kindergarten teacher becomes aware that a child in her room holds a prejudice against another, she devises some situation which will involve the two children in a shared activity so engrossing that the prejudice is forgotten in their desire to help each other. One day she was rewarded to see two little girls, from vastly different cultural and ethnic backgrounds, deeply absorbed in play. They were exchanging purses, as a result of their new-found friendship and affection. One purse was grubby, worn and shapeless, the other was new and shining. Each little girl was genuinely happy with the gift from her friend.

Role-playing and Dramatization

The opportunities for teaching good citizenship and self-discipline by using role-playing and dramatization are limitless. They could be used in any or all of the children-planned activities listed in this chapter. Young children often assume roles in their play which are enlightening and amusing. An adult, whether parent or teacher, has only to listen to a group of children playing school or "keeping house" to hear childish and often exaggerated versions of her own teaching.

Teachers can employ role-playing and dramatization to help children acquire self-control, to develop confidence in the shy child, to give the slow learner a feeling of achievement. In one kindergarten a retarded child, with little speech, always played roles as inanimate objects and his classmates were generous in their praise of him. He was delighted when a child told him, "You're the very best tree we *ever* had in *Tigers in the Jungle*. I'll bet you get choosed again."

When kindergartners have learned independence of thought and action, when they are able to accept responsibility, when they can judge their playmates on their worth, rather than color, family, or social position, they are beginning to become good citizens. When they are "training the self in behaviors that are acceptable . . . ," when they "can sublimate the needs of self to the needs of the group," they are beginning to acquire self-discipline.

3

The Teaching of
Music, Art and Other
Subjects in the
Kindergarten

Music in the Kindergarten

Music is an important part of the kindergarten program, but it is often one of the most neglected activities. A teacher may say, "I have no talent in music. I am not an accomplished musician. I can scarcely carry a tune. I can't teach music well, so why bother!"

There are effective ways to teach kindergarten music which do not require great musical skill on the part of the teacher. All kindergarten teachers should be able to read music, however, so they can play simple tunes on the piano. If a teacher feels that she cannot accompany her students as they sing, she can pick out the melody of a new song and let the children hum it with her until the good singers have learned the tune. They can then help the others, and the teacher's participation can be reduced to a minimum.

The kindergarten teacher needs to examine many music books

which have been written especially for young children. From them she can choose songs to accompany units of study interests whenever possible. She will want to teach a variety of songs, and give every child an opportunity to play in a rhythm band. Children enjoy records, and will bring in many of their favorites. Listening to *good* records is an excellent experience for young children. But the teacher should be wise in her choice of the records her children listen to at school, and when possible she should build up her own library of school-provided records for games and listening experiences.

Children who cannot be successful in other kindergarten activities often enjoy music and sing very well. Many children, however, have no desire to sing when they enter kindergarten and are completely indifferent to all music activities. These disinterested children, when properly motivated, can become so interested and involved in music that they will *ask* to sing.

This book will discuss in detail one successful way to teach music in the kindergarten. The method involves every child's participation in either a vocal or physical way: hopefully most children will become interested in both ways to enjoy music.

Listening to music or singing words set to music does not appeal to every young child. Rhythms bore some children and they simply ignore all the wiles an anxious teacher may employ to get every member in her little group participating in a good time with songs and rhythms. To have Junior sit, day after day, as immovable and unblinking as a Buddha and completely indifferent to all the joyous (if not always beautiful) music around him, is apt to shatter the nerves of the most experienced teacher. Somehow it doesn't seem natural for a child to dislike music. If the teacher tries hard enough, and uses the right methods to intrigue his interest, *someday* even little Junior will burst into song! It may be a fearsome noise, or a monotone that hurts the ears, but Junior will sing at last, and *like* it!

All songs used in kindergarten should be gay, with tunes that are pleasing and pitched so that children's voices can easily reach the highest notes. A few children may have high voices, but most children dislike songs that have high notes they cannot easily reach, and they refuse to sing those songs.

Kindergarten songs should have words that rhyme and words whose meanings are easily understood by children. It is distracting when a teacher has to stop and explain that the word "hue" in a song means color and *not* that boy, Hugh, in second grade, whom everybody hates!

When possible, songs in kindergarten should concern children's interests, units of study, seasonal events, holidays, all the many things that claim the attention and interest of young children. Many new songs should be taught throughout the school year. The old favorites can be enjoyed by the group, from time to time, in a free choice of all-the-songs-we've-learned-this-year songfest; but new songs, which are carefully chosen and well taught, can help to intrigue the interest of every child in the room, including little Junior who doesn't like music.

Songs which are kindergarten favorites offer *more* than a sweet tune and easily understood words. They offer physical participation, or perhaps counting experiences. Boys and girls like songs that lend themselves to competition in singing. The ingenious teacher can devise many ways to make music a joyous experience, even for the child who might be tone deaf; certainly she can be sure that every child will like *some* of the songs some of the time.

Music releases tensions, relaxes inhibitions, helps young children to forget shyness, anger and frustrations. Dramatic play can so easily be used in the enjoyment of songs. The teacher can encourage the children to interpret songs in dramatic play, always wisely preventing the unrestrained hilarity that can sometimes spoil a group's physical participation in any activity.

Some kindergarten songs lend themselves to a "You sing the question, I'll sing the answer" type of participation. Both boys and girls love this sort of song-game, and every child always enters into the fun. One such song, made up by the kindergartners themselves, began as a train song, and the words were sung to the tune of *London Bridge Is Falling Down*. Sometimes the boys sang the questions and the girls answered, and then they would reverse singing roles.

Question:
"How does the freight train transport food?

"Transport food?
"Transport food?
"How does the freight train transport food?"

Answer:
"In the refrigerator car."

The questions varied to include hopper, cattle car, box car, flat car, oil tanker, caboose, tender, engine, roundhouse, etc. as correct answers. In learning about passenger trains the questions and answers involved conductor, dining car, pullman coach, and observation car.

Children enjoy using the "question and answer" type of song to highlight other studies and interests, and they may want to choose another familiar tune. "Where does a hamster carry food?" or "Where does a caterpillar spend the winter?" are nature questions. Kindergartners are ingenious at asking questions which involve number concepts, too.

Another song, an adapted German folk tune, *We're Going on the Train*[1] is an excellent one to involve the shy or indifferent child in music enjoyment. It has a simple tune but it is the most beloved and most frequently chosen tune, when one kindergarten group studies transportation. The reason? It "takes" each child, by name, on a train ride, in groups of four children to a car. It allows each child to be mentioned personally. When his own name is called each little John or Mary ducks a head, grins, and wriggles with pleasure. The song has to be repeated over and over until each child is aboard the train, and in large kindergarten groups of over forty, that takes a long time! Their teacher may get weary of the song, but the children never tire of it. It is a simple song, a simple device to interest every child in the class; but it is one hundred percent effective, and an unqualified favorite!

Another song in the same book was found to be more fun to *say* than to *sing,* because its words were so delightful. *The Railroad Train*[2] was used by the teacher as a speech-teaching device,

---

[1] Laura Pendleton MacCarteney, *Songs for the Nursery School* (Cincinnati, Ohio: Willis Music Company).
[2] *Ibid.*

to challenge those children who had lazy tongues, babyish speech or more serious speech defects. The teacher showed her children how lively their tongues must be as they "clickety-clacked" and "alunked" along the track. She discussed with them how many tricks the tongue must do as it formed the words of this poem-song. While they enjoyed the ways the words "felt" in their mouths they all talked together about *other* sounds which were made with tongue, teeth, lips and breath. All the children delighted in the tongue-twisting words of *The Railroad Train* and in the rhythm of its lines. There were other good features about the song. It served as an excellent way to talk about safety, too. It instructed the modern child in the steam engine, which is seen so seldom now.

There are many excellent books for the teaching of kindergarten music and this author has used many of them. One series of books lends itself to the teaching-of-music-with-physical-participation method discussed in this chapter. *Singing Fun* and *More Singing Fun*[3] are books which include many songs that are not only delightful to sing but can be used for other learning experiences such as number combinations, names-of-things, dramatizations and speech activities. The following songs from *Singing Fun* are excellent ones. "I Wiggle" is effective to use at the beginning of school as an activity for children who have a short attention span and are tired and restless. "The Singing Farm" can be used for dramatization. "Ten Yellow Chicks" can be used as a counting experience by prolonging it to count "One yellow chick, Two yellow chicks," etc. Other counting songs are "Five Little Firemen" and "How Many People Live at Your House?"

"Ten Little Jingle Bells" and "Ten Little Froggies" are songs which can be used as physical-activity learning experiences, teaching combinations of ten. Ten children stand in a row, for the jingle bells that hung in a row. As the song proceeds through ten there are no children standing, the bells in the snow are counted each time, the bells still hanging are counted and combinations of ten are easily understood. The counting experience is

---

[3] Lucille Wood and Louise Binder Scott, *Singing Fun* and *More Singing Fun* (Manchester, Missouri: Webster Division, McGraw-Hill Book Company).

doubly meaningful because the gay song and the bodily movement accompany it. Later, in Math, when these children talk about all the ways to say the number ten, they easily remember those combinations of 2 and 8, 3 and 7, 4 and 6, 1 and 9.

"Ten Little Froggies," used in the spring and fall with nature study of frogs and toads, is a jolly, delightful, jump-in-the-pool song with physical activity and it, too, is used as a math experience.

"The Little White Rabbit Who Wanted Red Wings" is a folk tale which lends itself to all kinds of experiences for young children, dramatizations, the practice of responses to questions, the opportunity to create costumes. In a music activity like this one there are so many excellent opportunities for children to work together in groups, to share ideas, to make decisions and pass judgments. Every child will find some task at which he can succeed. Even monotones who do not sing well may be very clever at drama, in devising stage settings and creating costumes.

More Singing Fun[4] offers Halloween songs, transportation songs and many songs which lend themselves to math experiences, such as "Christmas Counting Song," "How Many Snowflakes?," "Four Robins," and "Five Kites." "Three Polliwogs" is a good song to teach with a nature unit, "An American" with a study unit on being a good citizen.

In planning her music program the kindergarten teacher will want to make music as interesting and as attractive as possible to both girls and boys. She can choose songs from sources at her disposal that are seasonal, that are easy to teach and sing, that create interest in some special unit of study.

Rhythms are an important part of the kindergarten music program. Participation in a rhythm band, with whatever instruments are available, is a rewarding experience for most children, particularly for those who cannot achieve success in other activities.

Kindergarten teachers can make many rhythm instruments, with the children's help. Large coffee cans, with old inner-tube

---

[4] Lucille Wood and Louise Binder Scott, *More Singing Fun* (Manchester, Missouri: Webster Division, McGraw-Hill Book Company).

pieces stretched across the ends, make very good Indian drums. (The inner tubes are hard to find now, but are available.) Other materials may be used for the ends of drums, such as imitation leather, the plastic covers that are furnished with coffee cans, heavy oiled paper, and real leather if a teacher can be lucky enough to get remnants from some factory. Beaters for the drums can be made by cutting dowel sticks into nine-inch lengths and buying enough rubber crutch tips to fit one on the end of each stick.

When rhythm sticks are not available to the teacher, blocks may be clapped together. Rattles can be made by putting aluminum *Dip* containers together, or small aluminum pie tins, with beans or rice inside. Children can sew the tins together, using large needles and string. (Yarn is prettier and more colorful but breaks after several vigorous usings.) Small bells, for sale in the stores in the Christmas season, may be sewed on these rattles or may be sewed on a single tin or cardboard box. The ingenious teacher can devise other musical instruments which will serve very well in a rhythm band.

Creative Art in the Kindergarten

In the early weeks of kindergarten some children may still make crayon scribbles on paper in an attempt to express an idea or thought. When a child talks about the scribbles he has made he may call them a dog, or a house. His teacher will not see the forms he says are there, but she *can* see that the child has made an image of something that has meaning for him. He has been creative without being skillful, but at this point in his development the picture he has made is his best effort and should be valued by his teacher.

The kindergartner may draw on his past experiences as he makes pictures, or he may portray the delightful fantasies which intrigue him. A creative teacher can find many ways in which to stimulate her kindergartners to expressions of their feelings by providing them with many new and interesting experiences. A story, a bit of verse, some unusual happening enjoyed by the group, will bring forth the most creative expressions of what each individual child *heard, saw* or *felt.* Each child will have his own things to say on paper.

Gay, rollicking words in a bit of nonsense verse delighted the children in one kindergarten. They not only wanted to learn the words but were eager to put the sound of them down on paper with crayons. The teacher suggested, "Close your eyes and listen to a story about Hennery Brown. When I finish the story, you may make a picture of Hennery."

> One night when I had gone to bed,
> An idea popped into my head.
> I got a pencil and wrote it down,
> It was the story of Hennery Brown.
> On a sunny day, as I walked to town,
> I met a man named Hennery Brown.
> This Hennery was the strangest fellow,
> His pants were purple, his shirt was yellow.
> His shoes were orange and his eyes were blue.
> His ears were *huge* and his mouth was, too.
> His nose was long and sometimes red,
> 'Cause he often stood upon his head.
> His hair was stringy and long and green,
> The greenest hair I have ever seen.
> He carried a cane that was big and black,
> As he walked it made a clickety-clack.
> Oh, he was funny, this Hennery Brown,
> The man I met as I walked to town.

The pictures of Hennery Brown (Figures 1 and 2) which some of the children made are individual expressions of their enjoyment of the rhyme and the things they saw, felt and heard when they listened to the story about him.

Other ways to motivate children's creative art expressions are by reading stories, by having dramatizations and by role-playing. After a nature study the children may want to put down their impressions of what they have seen and learned on paper with crayons or paint, or they may want to model them with clay. Music prompts some children to art expression, as they draw what they think or what their imaginations say to them. They

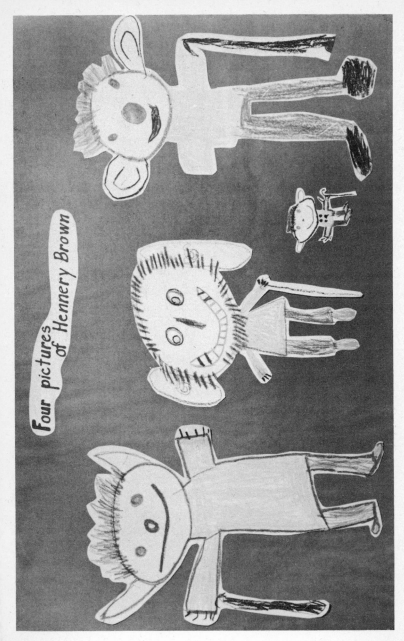

Figure 1.

Figure 2.

rely on emotional or social experiences and do not necessarily put down all that they have seen; they may, instead, draw what has most appealed to them. Whatever they make, they will have something to say.

Children need to work independently, to use their own ideas, to develop their own art-form concepts. The teacher will want to encourage each child, so that he may gain confidence in his ability to express himself. She should avoid comparing one child's work to that of another, or judging a child's work by adult standards. Kindergarten children sometimes judge each other's work quite cruelly, however, and "poke fun" at the child who is still expressing himself in large scribbles and blobs of color. Their teacher can help them to understand that a child's work is always highly valued as an expression of his individual creativeness, that differences in art are more valued here than conformity of shapes and designs.

Brant listened one day while his teacher was praising another child's picture, which he had proudly presented to her. "Danny, that picture is lovely, with such happy colors. Thank you for making it for me."

When Danny had walked away Brant, who continued to watch as his teacher studied the picture, suddenly accused her, "You don't think Danny's picture is pretty, because it ain't. It's messy! You only said that to make Danny feel good."

Brant's standards of art, unfortunately, were based on a play-school experience with many hectographed pictures; these he had been required to color with much keeping-within-the-lines instruction from adults. Like them Brant found pictures pretty only when they met certain standards of neatness and conformity. He had not yet learned the joy of expressing his thoughts and feelings in creative art.

When a child comes to kindergarten his world still revolves primarily around himself. The very immature child will draw only his head, with legs attached, perhaps; if the picture is one of himself in an inactive situation, he doesn't make the legs at all, because he doesn't need legs. As a child's experiences increase, as he observes his world, as he becomes aware of the ways in which other children express themselves, his own work changes. He occasionally draws in great detail. If he is a child with what is called "native ability," and can make his pictures attain some degree of photographic reproduction, the result is sometimes frank and startling.

Gino, while taking a reading-readiness test at the end of his kindergarten year, was asked, for test purposes, to draw a penciled picture of himself. He did, making a very recognizable picture of a boy, fully clothed, but with sex organs drawn in, too. When questioned he said, "Sure, I've got my clothes on in my picture. But that's what I look like inside. All boys look like that inside their clothes. My dad says so." (This type of x-ray picture is sometimes made by second- or third-graders, but *rarely* by a kindergartner.)

When children have achieved some type of simple form concepts, the kindergarten teacher may then have discussions with them about things they have seen or done, or about things they would like to see and do. Each child's picture, after such a discussion, is an expression of his own ideas and enthusiasm about the project.

After children have shared a common experience, like an exciting bus trip to the zoo, their impressions of what they did and saw are widely diversified. One child may have found the bus trip itself more exciting than the zoo animals. When he makes his picture of the zoo trip, a yellow bus is predominant. Another child may have found that feeding peanuts to the bears was the highlight of his trip, so his picture may show his hand with some peanuts on the palm. He doesn't make a picture of the bears at all, merely of his *hand feeding* the bears. Each child's interpretation of the trip to the zoo is right for him, because each picture portrays what the individual saw and felt.

Emphasis, in recent years, has been on developing children's creativeness in all areas of learning. The kindergarten teacher, in order to encourage complete creativeness in art, must discard all her previous ideas of standardized achievement and allow each child's art work to be a true expression of himself.

Social Studies

Learning about other people and how they live is an exciting experience for young children; learning about themselves and the people that are involved in their own lives is equally engrossing. Learning how to be a good citizen, how to make valuable contributions to their own community is easily within the comprehension of five-to-six-year-olds. Study units about social living, which have been developed from children's curiosity and interest, with their varied learning objectives are presented in detail in Chapters 9, 10 and 11 in this book.

Meaningful Math

Most kindergarten teachers have their own approved and accepted methods of presenting number concepts which have been decided upon by their own school system, so this book will not discuss the subject in detail. Whether a teacher uses new math methods, a simple number workbook, or considers number concepts concerned with numerals 1 to 10 as sufficient background for first grade is, of course, a matter of school policy.

There are several important objectives for teaching a mathematics program in kindergarten, however: number meanings from one to ten, an understanding of one-to-one relationships and simple mathematical terms, and an understanding of the way mathematics is used in their daily lives are perhaps the main objectives in a program planned for young children. Concepts of space, measurement, time and money can be introduced along with interesting study projects and will be doubly meaningful as the children learn to make practical uses of new knowledge; as they play store and make change, or construct objects from materials which they have measured themselves. Detailed examples of ways in which kindergarten teachers may correlate mathematics with units of interests in other subjects, and games that teach number concepts are presented in Chapters 10 and 11.

Meaningful math can be experienced in and related to every activity in the kindergarten. The teacher can plan to involve her children in everyday relationships which deal with numbers of things. "How many sheets of drawing paper do you need for the children at the *first* table? At the *second* table? At the *third* table?" "Please bring me five triangles." "We have nine girls at this table. Two girls do not want milk this morning. How many boxes of milk will you need to bring?" "Alice, please pass out these napkins and tell me how many more you will need for the children at your table." "Ten children at the first table may go to the right side of the room. Ten children from the second table may go to the left side of the room." "Today will be the last day of school this week." "We will have four school days and one weekend before our holiday. How many days are there in a weekend?" "How many days all together will we have before our holiday?" "Our rest time will begin when the big clock hand is on 6. We will finish resting when the big clock hand is on 9." "Here is a piece of chalk. I will give chalk to four children. Show me how to divide this piece of chalk." These and countless other directions and questions involve the children in simple number associations. Opportunities in kindergarten for teaching the understanding of numbers are unlimited.

Nature and the World Around Us

Nature is a word that encompasses the large area of a child's senses and the wonders he can discover and experience with them. The city child is somewhat handicapped in the study of nature when he seldom sees flowers growing wild, never sees trees, grass or the wild creatures that live in fields, woods, and streams. His teacher must help him to experience Nature's wonders by intensifying those experiences he *can* have in his limited environment. She must try to provide additional experiences in the kindergarten room which will appeal to the child's sight, smell, touch, hearing and taste. If school rules permit she can have small caged animals in the room, which the children can care for and observe. Aquariums, an ant farm, planted seeds and flowering plants all help to bring nature into the schoolroom. City children can observe and keep records of the weather, observe clouds and learn about snowflakes.

The city child may grow to adulthood without having waded in a stream, looked in big-eyed surprise at a nest of furry bunnies under a fence row, smelled the fragrance of a pine forest and scuffed bare feet through thick pine needles. All this is regrettable, but the city child can still learn about nature from pictures, from stories, from pets and growing things in the schoolroom. Most adults have not and will never experience a trip in a space ship, yet most interested adults can acquire a satisfying knowledge of the present exciting space program. Teachers in city schools, then, have the responsibility of creating a world of nature for their children and of making that world as exciting as possible.

For the school child who can visit the country, who can see living wild creatures of the earth and air around him, nature can be a joyous, personal experience. He can learn about animal babies, animal homes, bird homes, the habits of wild creatures. He learns how the tadpole turns into a frog by watching the gradual process in a tank in his kindergarten room, when some fortunate boy has had the fun of accompanying his dad down to the pond to *collect* the tadpoles. Children can watch a caterpillar, which has been found in the woods and kept in a wire cage, spin its chrysalis or cocoon. In due time he can watch it emerge into a breathtaking beauty, as a butterfly or moth, and start its new life as a far different sort of creature from the one the child knew as a caterpillar. He can follow an animal's tracks in the sand or snow and learn to identify the animal by the tracks. He can make an impression of a track with plaster of paris, and keep it to talk about and display; he can watch a sea creature or a fresh-water crayfish scurrying about in its shell and realize that nature's creatures are always exciting to the sight, smell, touch, hearing, even taste of a child.

A little boy, during an engrossing study of shells, was looking intently at the picture of a large clam, which was being forced open by a starfish. The kindergarten class had participated in a lively discussion about the picture and the habits of starfish, which feed upon other shell creatures. They knew that a strong man would have difficulty opening the large clam with his hands, but the starfish, who needed it for food, was somehow strong enough to force the clam to open so it could eat the flesh inside. Skip looked at the picture, then at his teacher. "I know just how that clam sounded when the starfish forced it open," he said.

"You do? How did it sound?"

"It went eeeeeeeeeee, like a squeaking door that opens slow on rusty hinges."

An experience that challenges the imagination, calling on facts learned by personal contact or from interesting material which has been presented in an appealing way, creates the most receptive learning atmosphere in the kindergarten.

Field trips are a wonderful learning experience. Trips to the farm, to the zoo, a bakery, any place of interest which a community has to offer, should give a child much to think and talk about. An excursion into the woods in the spring will bring the joy of finding wild strawberry plants, small wild flowers, delicate moss or mushrooms. After a trip to the farm the children in one kindergarten discussed all the babies they had seen, and the way in which they had come to life, some being hatched from eggs, like the fluffy baby chickens and ducklings, some emerging from their mothers' bodies, like the kittens and small pink pigs they had loved so much. The children made pictures of the things they had seen on the trip that interested them most. Alvy, a city child who had recently moved to the community, had been very excited at the sight of live animal babies. He brought his picture proudly to his teacher. "See this?" he said, his brown eyes sparkling. "That's the mama pig and these are her little babies. And these," he explained, pointing to the small objects in the corner of the picture, "are the pig eggs that didn't hatch!"

Science

The young child comes to school with a great zest for living and a tremendous curiosity about the world in which he lives. Science helps him to find answers to his questions by exploring, observing, investigating, experimenting and handling, by using all his senses. Science helps the young child to new knowledge of *ways* to find out the answers to his questions. He should be allowed to find out for himself about the sizes of things, the shapes of things and the textures of objects. He wants to feel their hotness and coldness. The young child will want to know why things sometimes change their shapes, sizes or textures. He must have many firsthand experiences and be allowed to investigate objects and materials and make observations about them. One of the chief purposes of science study is to alert the child to the satisfaction of learning about the world around him; to alert him to the reason *why* things happen as they do. He must be aware of his own ability to contribute to changes in his environment.

The kindergarten child is eager to learn about moving air, the moisture in air and how it behaves, about clouds, soil, the contour of the land; of sand, stones and big rocks, and water in its many forms. He should have answers to his questions in words he can understand, or in experiments he can share. He is an earnest, eager listener and worker who wants and needs to know the reasons why things happen as they do.

Young children should be provided with simple, fundamental tools such as magnifying glasses, yardsticks and rulers. They need various kinds of measures for quantity, and a scale of simple balance. They will want to experiment with magnets, to rig up small machines. Their teacher should gather together all materials needed by her kindergartners so that their experiments may be interesting and meaningful. These simple materials are seldom expensive, and parents will often contribute materials, if they are asked to help with a project.

Parents will want to be involved in science activities, if given the opportunity. Interesting science experiments can be presented as a demonstration to the class, with a kindergarten child–dad team explaining the procedure. Not only is a demonstration of this nature valuable to the children who share it, but it may be a means to involve the interest of many other fathers in school activities. Mothers and grandmothers can instruct young children in simple cooking and sewing activities, and they will enjoy working with the kindergartners. Children are very happy when a member of their family contributes something interesting to their group.

Kindergartners should be allowed to learn, by experiment, that they can't always trust their senses but should *prove* that a thing is so before they call it so. They must learn to gather all facts together to be considered before they can arrive at a positive conclusion. Games of all kinds can be planned by the teacher to test the children's credulity, to challenge their deductive reasoning and to help them acquire the habit of inductive reasoning. They must learn to seek for positive proof of a truth. All red things are not apples, all apples are not red; all furry things are not animals, and all animals are not furry. Any simple experience can spark a group's involvement in science.

To many young children the things that happen around them are magic. Some adults once provided a kindergarten class with a magician's program and were quite disconcerted when the children received the program enthusiastically but with no amazement at the magical tricks. To a young child, whose whole world is made up of unbelievably delightful happenings, everything is accepted. A rabbit in a hat is no more surprising than the sun's warmth that burns a tender skin in summer; no more incredible than the appearance of new leaves on bare branches in the spring. He accepts the fact that moisture *disappears* from a freshly washed blackboard, and moisture *appears* on the outside of a pitcher of ice water in a very warm room. All these things are akin to magic. Flowers suddenly emerging from the magician's wand are not so exciting as the legs that emerge from a tadpole's body as he gradually becomes a frog before the child's very eyes. Magic permeates the child's whole world and science can be the key to unlock its fascination.

Science in the kindergarten can be a wonderful experience, with experiments of all kinds giving opportunities for investigation and exploration. What a wise teacher she is who provides the simple tools and materials with which children can work, and the willingness to let them touch, taste, smell, look, listen and learn-by-doing!

Foreign Language

When five-year-olds come to school everything is a new and unexplored experience. A foreign language fits very easily and naturally into their daily program of social living and learning, which involves number experiences, reading-readiness, dramatizations, stories, etc.

In one kindergarten Spanish was taught to both afternoon and morning classes for many years. The first introduction to the language began with Spanish greetings and goodbyes. By Friday of the first school week the kindergartners were reminded by their teacher that "Hasta manana" was *not* a proper way in which to tell them goodbye today, as she would not see them for several days; instead, they exchanged the greeting "Hasta la vista." On each succeeding Friday for the remainder of the year, the children always remembered not to say "Hasta manana."

By the end of the first week of school preferences for chocolate or white milk were requested in Spanish, the Spanish color names for the American flag were learned. Later, Spanish names for all colors were learned and the children played many delightful games with color names, colored paper, and colored objects in the room. The names of numerals, one to ten, were easily learned, and daily attendance was taken in Spanish. As the attendance was large, the kindergartners soon learned to count to thirty and five, forty and five, twenty and eight, depending on children present. They enjoyed counting songs, like the Spanish version of "Ten Little Indians." Counting beyond fifteen helped them to comprehend number values in English, too. Some small children had not realized that sixteen, seventeen and eighteen literally meant six and ten, seven and ten, eight and ten. Counting became a fascinating experience. Before long some children were begging, "Please help us to learn to count to a hundred in Spanish."

Names of objects in the room were learned and good manners were stressed. Children who forgot to say "please" and "thank you" soon learned to say "por favor," "muchas gracias" and "de nada." Name games delighted them. One child might ask members of the group, "¿Como se llama usted?" and after a few times each child would reply with the Spanish version of his own name, Ricardo, Maria Elena, Jorge, Pedro, Catalina or Rosita.

Sometimes their teacher would ask, "¿Cuantos anos tiene usted?" to which the children would answer, "Yo tengo cinco anos" or sometimes very alert children would tease and answer, "I am ten years old" which would bring much laughter. Kindergarten children love the obvious joke. Even the not-so-quick child would catch on, and struggle valiantly to make a calculated wrong answer and get a laugh.

Spanish directions were given, and games were played in Spanish which taught the following of directions in sequence, and the retention of many directions in sequence. The directions often used the Spanish words for colors, objects and numbers of things, such as, "You may get two pencils, three pink papers, one red book, one black telephone and one grey eraser." "You may touch the door, the window, Richard's chair, Mary's red shoes." In this way the child was forced to think in Spanish, for he must remember names, colors, numbers, commands and the sequence of the commands, all in Spanish, a language which had been unknown to him before he entered kindergarten.

The flannel board was used to teach spatial relationships, small, medium and large concepts. It was used, too, to tell illustrated stories, with the flannel characters portraying the action while the story was told or read in Spanish. There are many delightful books which tell stories in Spanish. These were all great favorites with the children.

In these kindergarten classes nothing was ever said about learning a foreign language. The first Spanish words were introduced into the program as naturally as any other words, they were used in everyday activities, each new word was received as casually by the children as they would receive a new English word. When a child came from home with a request, "Tell me the Spanish word for secretary, my father wants to know," the teacher and the child consulted the Spanish dictionary together. These kindergarten children were taught that books are a source of knowledge, to be consulted when needed and they yearned to read the words, as well as the pictures. Their introduction to a foreign language proved to be a very enjoyable experience. True, some children could not pronounce the words well, but some five-to-sixes can't pronounce English words correctly, either. As children went further into Spanish study in first grade through junior and senior high school many of them recalled their first knowledge of Spanish in kindergarten with real pleasure.

4

Units of Study which Employ
Projects, Techniques
and Subject Materials
that Appeal
to a Child's Senses

Kindergarten children approach new activities with their own individual interests in mind. They make their contributions to those activities from the knowledge they have already acquired from preschool investigating, experimenting, exploring and observing. Curiosity is natural to the young child. When he enters kindergarten he has already learned to seek answers to many of his questions in his play, by manipulation of objects, by examination and comparison, by evaluation from his own point of reference. His kindergarten teacher will stimulate his curiosity by offering opportunities for answer-seeking in the program she plans for her students. She knows that a child can become so absorbed in a school activity which interests him that his attention will be sustained for steadily lengthening periods of time.

The teacher capitalizes on the varied interests of her kindergartners when she encourages their observations, discussions and experiments. She realizes that all children will not learn the same things from identical experiences, but each child has his own questions which he wants answered. Creative thinking and problem solving are the delightful and rewarding results of activities which are prompted by the child's own interests. Activities, developed by the group, which involve every-member participation, give each child a pride in achievement which pleases and satisfies him. The richness and variety of his own experiences and his *personal* involvement in any project make it educationally significant for him. Learning becomes more vivid and pleasant when a child's senses are involved, so the kindergarten teacher helps her children plan ways to include sense perception experiences of seeing, hearing, touching, smelling, sometimes even tasting.

NATURE

Moths and Butterflies

These are some questions which young children want answered in a study of moths and butterflies:

> What is it?
> Where did it come from?
> How do I know it's a moth?
> What is the difference between a moth and a butterfly?
> Does it have a home like a bird or an animal?
> What does it eat?
> How many legs does it have?
> Is it useful to people?
> What kind of babies does it have?
> Can you find moths and butterflies everywhere?
> Are moths and butterflies found in cities? On the mountains? Over the ocean?

In wooded areas, or in areas where shrubs and flowers are grown, both in town and city, children may find and closely observe moths, butterflies and insects of all kinds. Kindergarten children enjoy making collections of insects. They will bring in both living and dead specimens of butterflies, caterpillars, even cocoons or chrysalises. When they have learned where to look for these creatures, small children seem to be more adept at locating specimens than adults. Their bright eyes and close proximity to the ground make it possible to see the lovely chrysalis of the monarch butterfly as it hangs from a fence rail or the branch of a milkweed plant. They find a fat moth cocoon among leaves or on the naked branches of bush or tree. The large, horned caterpillar of the Sphinx moth or the bristly caterpillar of a Mourning Cloak butterfly may be captured and brought to school in a jar.

When a captured caterpillar specimen spins its cocoon in the classroom, before the eyes of the astonished kindergartners, they have watched one of nature's wonders. They watch the horned caterpillar burrow into the earth they have provided, then later uncover it to find that it has changed into its new, hard brown chrysalis form; that the shape of the wings it will later have, as a Sphinx moth, are clearly visible (as well as the long sucking tube on the tomato-Sphinx chrysalis). Observation of this creature's metamorphosis is a wonderful learning experience.

It is exciting for children to watch a large monarch butterfly emerge from its rather small chrysalis. At first its wings are damp and flaccid, but they grow strong as the kindergartners watch. Soon the butterfly is poised for flight.

They watch with intense interest as the firm, leaf-wrapped cocoon of a Polyphemus moth, which has hung on their bulletin board all winter, suddenly begins to tremble with the activity of the creature inside. A hole appears and perhaps a drop or so of chalky liquid in one end of the hard cocoon. Presently a creature with a huge body and large, wet wings emerges through that hole. The children watch with excitement as the creature's fuzzy feet climb upon the sturdy branch they have provided. There it hangs, and they see it slowly pumping liquid from its swollen body into its beautifully marked big wings. As its body becomes thinner, the moth flutters about in its new world, while the kindergartners ask dozens of questions about the process which they have observed; about this strange, beautiful new creature that was once a not-very-pretty caterpillar, and then a dull, leaf-wrapped cocoon in their room.

At last, when it is strong enough, the Polyphemus moth poises on a window sill of the classroom. The kindergartners seem to share its ecstasy as it becomes airborne and flies away.

One little girl, who had held the lovely creature on her hand, sighed as she watched the moth disappear into the trees. "It was the wonderfulest feeling when its little feet crawled up my arm!" she told her classmates.

Another child voiced the desire of the class when he said, "I would like to make a moth picture to show my mother. I'll make her one *just like that!*"

When the moth pictures were made on paper with a choice of crayons or paints, each picture vividly portrayed what the artist saw when he looked at the moth. The pictures were all bright, beautiful and completely different. They were the creative expression of the children's enjoyment in an exciting learning experience.

As they learn about moths, butterflies and insects, handle them, closely observe them and discuss them, there are many experiences young children may have in sensory perception. They feel the coverings of caterpillars and the jointed bodies of insects, they delight in having the creatures crawl over their fingers or along their arms. As they gather the correct leaf foods for each type of caterpillar they feel the texture of those leaves; the fuzzy surface of the milkweed plant and the sticky substance which oozes out when its stems are broken; they smell its distinctive odor. They slide their fingers over the smooth leaf of birch or poplar, which they gather for the Mourning Cloak caterpillar; they smell the rank odor of tomato vines as they gather food for the already-fat tomato-Sphinx caterpillar.

Children compare the slender bodies and antennas of butterflies with those of moths, whose bodies are heavy and seem to be covered with soft, sometimes brightly patterned fur. They look at wings through a magnifying glass and discover they, too, have textures, too delicate to be felt by little fingers. They learn that the feathery antenna of a large male moth not only distinguishes him from the female, but serves the purpose of helping him to find the female, even when they are separated by long distances.

Kindergartners are quite astonished to learn that some species of moths have no mouths for feeding, live only long enough to lay their eggs, and then die.

One concerned little girl asked, "You mean those mother moths don't take care of their own babies?" She was reminded that a female moth lays her eggs upon the right kind of plant, whose leaves will furnish proper food for the tiny caterpillars when they hatch from her eggs, so she really "takes care" of her babies, without being with them.

In one kindergarten room a live female Polyphemus moth was captured and brought to school. They watched her lay her round eggs on the screen-wire walls of an insect cage. Later on they were amazed when tiny black caterpillars emerged from the eggs. They eagerly provided oak, hickory, elm, maple, birch and other leaves as food for the tiny caterpillars.

"They don't look much like their mama," a little boy observed. The caterpillars shed their skins and changed in appearance as they grew larger, finally becoming large green creatures with segmented bodies and enormous appetites.

The kindergartners learned that caterpillars shed their skins as they grow, just as boys and girls outgrow their clothes. Growing their *own* caterpillars was a wonderful experience.

Other insects may be studied, along with moths and butterflies. The walking stick is an interesting insect which shows a child quite plainly how nature camouflages some of her creatures, so that they cannot be found easily. Children are fascinated by insects and their habits. They count their legs and watch the ways in which they use them to move about or procure food. They learn to identify the sounds made by many insects, not by using vocal cords as humans do, but by manipulating parts of their bodies.

There are many ways in which the senses can be involved in a moth, butterfly or insect study. The teacher will also want to provide stories to read aloud, film strips to watch, and large pictures or posters to look at and talk about. Children enjoy making brightly painted or colored pictures of moths and butterflies and they may want to make mobiles. Learning all about moths, butterflies and insects is an absorbing activity.

Animals Have Strange Homes

A small girl came to school one morning with an exciting story to tell her class. She had gone camping with her family for three days. Their tent was pitched on the bank of a river. A large tree, hanging over the water, was the home of a mother raccoon and her four small babies. As the little girl described the animal family, her classmates became very eager to tell of animal homes they had seen in strange places. The lively discussions that day led to such interest in animals and their habits that a unit of study was developed.

Children volunteered to make "reports" on the habits of certain animals, and enlisted the help of their families in finding resource materials. They brought books from home and from the library. A large bulletin board was arranged, *Homes That Are Not Houses,* and its purpose was to illustrate facts they learned about strange animal homes.

Arranging that bulletin board offered opportunities for the kindergartners to look at and examine the textures of many objects. Wasp nests, honeycombs, spider webs, nests of all kinds, shells of sea creatures, turtle shells, holes in trees, cocoons, all were examined and discussed in detail. Books were read to the children and many film strips of animal homes, animal families and their ways were shown to them. New vocabulary words were introduced and used in the study. Members of the bee family were identified, with the function of each member in the hive clearly understood. All kinds, sizes and shapes of turtles were studied, their shells, their habits, the way their eggs were laid, and their young.

Before the study activity ended, the wide variety of strange *people* homes was thoroughly investigated, too, and the kindergartners arrived at some interesting conclusions about the ingenuity of all living creatures in making suitable shelters for themselves.

Figure 3.

Houses of the Sea

City children may never have seen any accumulation of water larger than dirty street puddles after a heavy rain; but they may have heard about rivers, lakes and seas. They are curious about large bodies of water and learning about them is an interesting experience.

If a kindergartner brings a large conch shell into the room and instructs his classmates to hold the shell to their ear and "listen to the sea" every child gets a look of wide-eyed wonder as he holds the pink-lined conch to his ear and hears the sound of the air in the intricately formed shell.

What is a sea? Was the shell ever alive? Where did it grow? Could it really swim? What kind of a creature lived in it? Is a shell creature like a turtle? Is it like a fishbowl snail? These and many other questions are asked by kindergartners in their need to know about the sea and the creatures, other than fish, which live in it. Do shells grow in rivers and lakes? Why is there salt in the sea? What do shells eat? Do shells have babies? Can shells help man? Are the creatures that live in shells good to eat?

The children run their fingers over the brightly colored inner surface, the rough, ridged outer surface of the conch shell. They have seen turtles, and turtles' coverings, but this is very unlike a turtle's shell. When they are shown a picture of the conch, when it is alive, and are told how it lives and feeds, they may agree that the creature is not as beautiful as the house it lives in, but they agree that a study of sea shells promises to be very exciting.

Children of all ages are intrigued by sea shells. A collection of shells in the room can offer endless joy as the children examine and discuss them. A unit of study about shells furnishes opportunities for many wonderful learning experiences. One small collection, a book about shells, even a single shell brought to school by a child, may prompt the interest of kindergartners to the extent that they develop a study unit about shells and the sea. The book *Houses of the Sea,* by Alice E. Goudey, was responsible for launching such a study in one kindergarten. As the project proceeded, specimens of shells appeared from various sources. Resource books were consulted, the kindergartners comparing and discussing pictures and specimens to make sure that the shells they had in their room exactly matched the picture in the book. They learned the names of many shells, and how to determine whether a shell was a univalve or a bivalve. They learned to know which shells, when alive, had edible creatures in them. They found it exciting to learn that the creatures who inhabited a species of cone shell (but *not* a cone found in the waters bordering the United States) could sting with a venom as deadly as that of a rattler.

Stories about shell divers fascinated them. Their teacher talked of collecting shells with the live creatures still in them, and they learned what must be done to prepare the shells for a collection. The kindergartners examined a long, strange, jointed, tough object which they were surprised to learn was the egg case of a left-handed whelk. The case was filled with countless tiny, perfectly formed left-handed whelks.

One child brought in a rock-like material, dredged from land in the Florida Everglades. It contained many sea shells and led to discussions about Florida land that was once under part of the sea. There were discussions about Florida's beaches being made of coral sand, or sand that is made of pulverized shells, and the way coral sand differs from sand that was once rock.

Words like dredging, bivalve, univalve, venom, poisonous, tides, operculum and all the shell names were added to the vocabularies of the kindergartners.

The study included talk of the best time to gather shells and about tides. What are tides? What are the reasons for tides? To kindergartners who were beginning to regard the moon as a familiar, not-too-awe-inspiring object, this talk of moon-governed tides was interesting and entirely credible. They did not always understand everything they were told when their questions were answered, but they listened with great interest and *continued* to ask questions.

To most children who live inland, shells are unknown and mysterious, so a study of shells is a very rewarding and absorbing activity.

Signs of the Seasons

Changes in their physical world always intrigue the interest of young children. They are eager to ask questions and to offer their own ideas about changes they observe in their world.

They want to talk about:

Changing seasons and how they affect trees, flowers, birds, animals, people.

Why do seasons change?

Do seasons change all over the United States?

What preparations do people make for changing seasons? Animals? Birds? Plants?

Why do some trees shed their leaves in the fall while pine trees do not?

There will be many questions asked which have not been listed, of course, for signs which tell of changing seasons and the seasons themselves differ widely in this country. A study of all seasons, or of one particular season, can include many interesting activities that young children enjoy. There is talk of the earth's travel around the sun, and the proximity of the earth to the sun at each time of the year. There is globe and map study, bird flyways, discussion of climates; it can include field trips into city parks or country woods to observe seasonal changes in trees and shrubs; it can include a talk of temperature and weather or a detailed study of these interests; it can make observation of the awakening of new life after a long winter. Such a study might go on throughout the school year in areas where fall, winter, and spring are definitely defined seasons, and where preparations must be made by residents of those areas for the changing seasons. The varied interests, projects, discussions and experiments which result from such a study unit will involve all of a child's senses and challenge his curiosity about his physical world.

We Learn About Snow

Young children are always curious about snow. If they live in an area where snowfalls are rare, each one is treasured; if they live in a state where there is snow on the ground from late fall until late spring, or snowfalls come intermittently, they enjoy wonderful experiences with snow. This snow-study interest discussed here is a suggested one for any area where snow falls and remains on the ground most of the winter.

Why do we have snow? Where does snow come from? How is it useful to us? Why are there parts of the United States where there is *never* snow? Why are there parts of the United States where there is *always* snow? Such questions as these make the study of snow very engrossing to a young child as he finds out the reasons for climate and how it affects people. He learns how snow is formed, and the shape of a snowflake. (He may even be taught how to cut a six-pointed snowflake, because snowflakes are *always* six-pointed.) He melts snow, then freezes the water back to ice and discusses the way a lot of snow makes only a small amount of water, but that same water, when frozen, takes up more space in a container than before it was frozen. The reasons why these things happen are discussed as other experiments with snow are enjoyed. The children conclude that melted snow can make moisture for plants. It can make things beautiful, and it can be useful in many ways; but it can also make extra work for man. Heavy snowfalls can be dangerous.

There are some excellent books about snow on the kindergarten level, books which discuss snow in the city and in the country. A list of these will be found in the bibliography at the end of the book.

Footprints in the Snow

In communities where children have access to wooded areas, the presence of animal tracks in the snow makes a fascinating study for young children. These books furnish interesting ways to identify animal tracks (*Who Is It?* by Zhenya Gay and *Who Goes There?*, a Wonder Book by Janet and Alex D'Amato). Children soon learn to recognize and identify the tracks of the deer, raccoon, rabbit, frog or bear. Even a city child, who may never have seen any of these animals, will enjoy finding the likenesses and differences in their pictured tracks.

Figure 4.

An interesting experiment, which kindergartners can do, is to mix plaster of paris and carefully smooth it into deep, well-defined dog or cat footprints. The hardened imprints will be treasured by the kindergartners.

They may want to compare their own shoe prints or hand prints in the snow. An interesting side study is to allow all the children to make a chart of their own thumb prints, by using a black ink pad. This chart can be displayed in the room. When the thumb prints are examined, the children discover for themselves that each print is distinctive in some way and unlike every other print.

The teacher may want to devise a matching game, so children may match a picture of an animal with the picture of its footprint. This might be done first as a group activity, then as an individual game, each child having his own paper to mark by drawing lines from the animal picture to the pictured footprint.

In the study of footprints children learn to use their powers of observation, to be aware of minute details of their physical world. They make comparisons between the delicate hand-like tracks of the raccoon and their own hand prints; the footprints of the bear and their own footprints. Some alert child will always conclude that man can be identified by his own tracks; and by those of the horse he rides; or by the tires of the car he drives! He may leave his fingerprints on objects he handles; thus, they conclude, "the bad guys in the world get captured." A kindergartner's curiosity is endless. He wants to know *about* everything and the reasons *for* everything.

Seeds and How They Travel

The round white head of a dandelion which has gone to seed in the late spring or the blowing seed from a milkweed pod in the fall may prompt an interesting study of seeds in either of those seasons. The following list suggests only a few of the many interesting facts about seeds, any one of which could be developed into an engrossing study unit:

1. Kinds of seeds. (This list will be endless and varied, to coincide with the part of the United States in which a

child lives. Children enjoy learning that the pine cone, coconut, acorn, and avocado seed produce their own kind, but are no more effective than a tiny seed like that of the petunia. Each reproduces itself when it is given the proper environment and food.)

2. Purposes of seeds: to produce plants which in turn produce more seeds.
3. Plants: parts of plants; fruits, their parts and purposes.
4. Ways in which seeds travel: by air, by being harvested and sent in packets around the country, by being carried by birds, in the fur of animals, etc.
5. Experiments with seeds: planting seeds; observing roots, stems, leaves of plants; predictions about plants; effect of water on plants (too little, too much, enough); effect of light or sunshine on plant (too little, too much, enough).
6. Study of mature plants grown from seeds.
7. Study of fruits (shapes, skins, seeds, products from).

There are interesting art projects which can be carried on while the study of seeds is claiming the attention of kindergartners. Seeds of all kinds have wonderfully interesting shapes and textures. They may be used, with glue, to make creative designs on cardboard or heavy paper. Young children have good ideas about arrangement and color when working on projects of this kind.

Seeds may be used in other ways. Corn may be popped, parched or pounded into coarse meal. Pumpkin seeds may be strung on twine for necklaces, or toasted and eaten. Sunflower seeds may also be eaten. Children may want to bring in products used in the home which they have learned are made from various plant seeds. Different kinds of seeds may be put into aluminum cheese containers, sealed and used for rattles. The children will be surprised to hear the different sounds the seeds make, because they are of different sizes and are not all equally firm. Teachers and children, in such a study, can have many ideas about additional ways in which to use seeds for creative projects.

SCIENCE

Wind and Weather

Kindergartners enjoy talking about the weather. They hear their parents discuss it; they listen to weather broadcasts on radio and television, although they may not understand much of what they hear. Sometimes they are made acutely aware of weather when a decided change interferes with a family plan for an outing or celebration.

At school a young child will want to record the daily weather conditions and teachers need to devise various picture charts which make this record attractive and easy to manipulate.

How much does a child really understand about the weather and the reasons for weather changes? How can he find answers to the questions he may want to ask about wind, fog, rain, sleet, snow, thunder, lightning, storms of all kinds, dew on the grass in the morning, frost on father's car in the morning?

A simple study of wind can be great fun for kindergartners. They may have simple mobiles in their room, which move very gently when there is little movement in the room, quite briskly when active running games are being played near them. Wind, then, is moving air and they can make "a little breeze" by waving a paper about, or moving their bodies from side to side. They may ask questions: Why does moving air from a fan cool the air? Why, when a person is sweating, does a fan make him feel cool? What does the moving air *do*?

These, and other questions, can be answered by discussions and experiments showing water evaporation into the air and the condensation of moisture on cool objects; water evaporation from the newly washed chalk board; the steam from a teakettle disappearing into the air. They have observed that sometimes, before a rain, the air feels "different, kind of funny" and that, they learn, is humid air. Moisture collects on cool objects, they discover, when a pitcher of ice water, in a very warm room, becomes covered with moisture. All these things a child can look at and think about, as he helps with experiments in his room. He acquires new words: evaporation, moisture, condensation, humidity. He begins to understand that dew does not "fall" like rain, as he may have thought, but results from moisture in the air and the cooling of objects. Children have experienced fog and they begin to get an idea of how clouds are formed when they realize that a fog is a ground cloud. Walking to school through a fog with the smell of rain in one's nostrils is fun, because they know that the experience is similar to having a cloud surround a person on a high mountain; they can imagine how a pilot in a plane feels when he flies through a cloud. When the child looks at a cloud in the sky, after such experiences, he has the satisfaction of knowing what that cloud is like. When he watches the movement of clouds across the sky he knows that there is wind, rapidly moving air, which causes them to scud along.

Some kindergartners fear storms, are terrified of lightning and thunder. Talking together about the reasons for lightning and thunder may not completely dispel those fears, but children are very interested in learning the reasons why things happen, and discussing storms somehow takes away their mysterious and frightening aspect.

The kindergarten teacher may want to keep the study of wind and weather a continuing one, with the children asking new questions and making observations throughout the school year, as each new season or weather change occurs. Seeking the answers to their questions, recording temperature changes, learning as much as they can about air, land and water, and the way they affect each other, will keep young children enthralled during the entire school year.

There are many factual and fiction books which a teacher can use as she guides her kindergartners in finding answers to their questions about weather. The film strips, *Land, Air and Water, The Air Around Us,* and *What Makes the Wind* are all excellent to use in such a study.

There are many things which children can construct in their study of wind and weather. Mobiles, sailboats, parachutes, planes, kites, whirl-arounds and simple windmills all add to the interest of the study. Bulletin boards, which furnish ways to record the new information they have acquired, offer every-member participation. Parents sometimes become interested in their child's enthusiasm and will put on demonstrations of some device or other to show the movement of wind, or the power which moving wind or water can generate.

What Do the Clouds Say?

A simple bulletin board, like the one pictured in Figure 5, which children can help to make, will serve as a guide to a day-by-day evaluation of what the clouds are telling us about the weather. The pictures are cut from an old text book, the clouds are made from cotton, colored with grey chalk; all are mounted on construction paper.

Kindergartners soon learn to understand and use the terms *cumulus* and *cirrus* when discussing clouds. Some of them will be able to remember the terms *strato-cumulus* and *nimbo-stratus*, when deciding whether the dark clouds are still drifting about and threatening rain or are genuine rain clouds.

Children become very observant and are often aware of the first cumulus cloud that appears in a clear blue sky. They enthusiastically watch as storm clouds clear away, after rain, and their world brightens, or as storm clouds scurry overhead and away, without rain.

Watching the weather and understanding a few simple reasons for weather changes makes children much more observant of the world in which they live. They realize that some things cannot be governed by man, while others can. Experiences of this kind help the young child to make intelligent evaluations of nature, from his own limited knowledge and experience; he begins to understand the ways in which a child like himself can be affected by wind, rainfall, sunshine, too much or too little water. Every phase of his life can become more meaningful, every sense more acutely aware of what he sees, hears, touches, feels, tastes and smells. He begins to comprehend why the food he eats, the clothes he must wear, the kind of shelter he needs are all governed by climate changes, and the location of his home in relation to the country in which he lives. He learns some of the ways in which man makes use of climate changes and adjusts to them.

WHAT DO THE CLOUDS SAY?

Cumulus clouds. Good Weather!

Cirrus clouds. It's windy!

Strato-cumulus clouds.
Hurry home! Rain is coming!

Nimbo-stratus cloud. It's raining!

Figure 5

Kindergartners, working on projects which appeal to their senses, learn to respect but also to evaluate each other's opinions. They learn to listen to others and to make interesting contributions of their own. They welcome each new interest as a challenging experience and soon learn where to find possible sources of information to help them develop their interests.

5

Creative Units
Developed
from
Group Interests

The units of study-interests for kindergartners, which are discussed in this chapter, have all been successfully developed in a classroom. Each area of learning resulted from diversified interests of heterogeneous groups of over thirty-seven five- to six-year-olds. While learning about a particular subject, the children suggested new ideas and approaches and asked new questions about relevant subjects which added excitement to the projects. These creative units of discovery and learning involved all children in the class, as they contributed on the level of their ability.

References will be made, when describing ways in which these units were developed, to songs, stories, reference books, film strips and other teaching aids, most of which are listed in the bibliography at the back of this book.

The interests of children vary, as their cultural and ethnic backgrounds vary. The author offers suggestions of ways in which the units presented in this chapter may be developed in other ways, from children's interests which widely differ from those of her participating groups.

We Are All Americans

A kindergarten group had just finished an engrossing study of Indians, our first Americans, when the subject of skin colors came up in class. A little girl observed, "Indians are supposed to have red skins, but I've seen lots of Indians when I travel with my mother and father. Their skins are kind of red, but really more like brown, like a squirrel is brown."

A Negro girl said, "I've got brown skin, but my brother's got black skin." A little boy broke in eagerly, "There's a kid in my Sunday school class, and he's got brown skin, too, but he's not a Negro. His mama used to live in Korea, and his daddy got married to her when he was a soldier. My mother told me." A girl with shining black hair giggled. "Me and my mother are Japanese," she announced. "Only my father says I'm really an American."

A lively discussion began, with everybody commenting on Americans and the colors of their skins. One little boy said, "We eat lots of times at a Chinese place and there's a Chinese boy there my size, but he's an American. He's my friend, and his skin ain't exactly like mine, but it's not exactly brown, neither."

So an interesting project got underway. The children carefully examined a stack of construction paper of many shades of tan and brown. Each child chose a shade and decided what kind of American child he would make, and what favorite American game or activity his child would be engaged in. From the discussion that resulted a unit began to develop, flexible as all kindergarten units of interest should be. The children showed a lively desire to know more about American children whose skins were different from theirs, whose homes were not like theirs, whose games might be unfamiliar to them.

Together the kindergartners and their teacher made their first chart, to help them answer all the questions they wanted to know about being Americans. They made many pictures to use with the chart, illustrating what they had already learned. One chart said:

WE ARE AMERICANS

Americans live in many kinds of houses.
Americans wear many kinds of clothes.
Americans have many colors of skins.
Americans have many colors of hair.

The kindergartners first learned that all children enjoyed stories and books, singing songs, playing with toys, playing games, learning about each other. They discussed Eskimos, Indians, all those Americans whose parents had originally come from China or Japan, Puerto Rico or Cuba, Mexico or Korea. They became involved in map study to discover where all those countries were located and why those people might want to settle in the United States. They studied the globe and talked about the differences in climate and how climate in the United States influenced the games children played, the clothes they wore, the food they ate, even the colors of their skins sometimes.

The concept of a child's environment was a new one for these young children, but it was presented in stories, pictures and discussions until they could understand how environment affected children and grown-ups.

They were delighted to discover that city children and country children, whatever their color, all enjoyed similar childish pleasures and interests; however, individual differences and likenesses in the appearances of children were discussed at some length. They made many pictures which were assembled in play groups, of American children having fun, flying kites, playing ball, walking their dogs, playing dolls, swimming and fishing.

From the discussion of school children the interest progressed to teachers who might have skins of many colors. One child had attended a school where his teacher was from Puerto Rico. The kindergartners talked of families and family fun, which brought up the subject of what families could or could not afford to do.

A lively study of economics was developed here. Why could some families afford things which others could not? How did

Figure 6.

American fathers support their families? Did the community in which they lived affect their fathers' ability to have good jobs? What did *they* think was a good job? (There were some enlightening answers here, amusing to an adult, but seriously considered by the kindergartners.)

An education, they decided, was important for fathers and mothers. Parents could never get good jobs without good educations. Did the colors of skins make a difference when fathers tried to get jobs? The children talked with their parents at home about many questions that interested them, and brought back reports about how their parents felt concerning educations, money and jobs.

The aid of parents was also enlisted when the children wanted some facts about famous Americans whose skins were brown or black. Pictures were brought in of many famous Negroes, Martin Luther King, the Postmaster of Chicago, Bill Cosby, Booker T. Washington, and many others. Prominent Indian men, on and away from their reservations, were discussed. The children learned how the life and habits of the Eskimos were changing and of ways in which the Eskimo fathers were being taught new skills so they could better provide for and educate their children.

The origin of the Hawaiian Islands was explained by their teacher in simple story form which introduced a new idea, the way the surface of the earth has changed and will continue to change. Comparisons were made between our two newest states, and their likenesses and differences were topics of conversation for days. Two beautiful picture maps, of Hawaii and Alaska, were used in the study. Stories, pictures, objects of art and new vocabulary words were introduced in the discussion. A small outrigger canoe was constructed, and the uses of outrigger canoes and the dugouts and canoes the Indians once used were discussed. How did they differ from the kayak used by the Eskimo? Why must the outrigger canoe and the kayak differ in construction from a canoe used on inland water?

An absorbing study of the flag was the next area of interest. One mother brought in an old flag with thirteen stars on its field. Comparisons were made between it and the present flag, with its fifty stars. Discussions and stories took the children back to colonial times to learn why the old flag had been made with thirteen stripes as well as thirteen stars.

The kindergartners, on their own initiative, brought in pictures of the President, Vice-President, the White House and the Capitol Building in Washington. They asked many questions about our government. Why did we have a vice-president? One very alert little boy asked who would be president if something happened to both the president and vice-president at the same time. (By this time the unit of interest, which was started because of children's curiosity about the colors of Americans' skins, was about to enter its eighth week of sustained and engrossed interest on the part of a heterogeneous group of thirty-eight children.)

Construction projects sustained the interest of those children who could not absorb all the factual material which was being offered by the study. Flags were drawn and colored, but the children who were not content to make their flags incorrectly, measured and spaced their stripes and colored them correctly. Outrigger canoes and kayaks were made from construction paper or balsa wood by those children who liked to work with their hands.

Upper-grade classes were guests in the kindergarten room to observe what was being learned there, and the children were delighted to share their new knowledge and use their new vocabulary words. By this time most of the children could identify matching words in their story charts, could discuss simple concepts of their President's duties, could talk intelligently about many phases of American life which differed vastly from their own. They understood simple facts about living in a country where it is not necessary to look alike, think alike or be alike. They had some conception of the privilege and obligation of being a citizen in the United States.

Eskimos

A very small boy came puffing into the kindergarten room and plopped a large, brown bag on a table. "That's the heaviest man I ever carried," he announced dramatically. There were cries of disbelief from his friends. "I have too got a man in there, an Eskimo man!" and he grinned in five-year-old triumph. The other children almost tore the bag to bits in their eagerness to see what was inside. It was indeed an Eskimo man carved from soapstone, and in his hand he held a harpoon. At his feet was a carved seal. The child explained that he and his family had just returned from his grandfather's home in Cleveland, Ohio. There he had met a real live Eskimo, who was his grandfather's friend. The Eskimo had carved the soapstone figures. "He gave me a real stuffed baby seal, too," he told the group. "But it smells. My mother said she'd bring it to show but she'd better take it right home after we see it."

The stuffed baby seal also visited school and questions about Eskimos and Eskimo life began to pop around the teacher like firecrackers. A little girl volunteered that her father had been stationed at a base in the north country where "he had his very own Eskimo dogs and sled." She would bring an album to school and show us pictures. Another child had a card sent to her from Alaska and on it was a baby husky's picture. A boy said he knew a family who had a really truly Eskimo husky, and it got an Eskimo sled for Christmas!

What was a husky?

That day we began to learn new vocabulary words and to plan for more talk about Eskimos and their lives. There were many books in our kindergarten library about Eskimos, all on the primary level, and these were first read to the children, then frequently consulted by them. The children loved the stories, and they soon realized that some stories told of a life that was now changing for Eskimo children, just as the lives of American children had changed "since the olden days." (These books are listed in the bibliography also, along with film strips which show the homes and habits of modern Eskimos.)

There were stories of seal and walrus hunting, fishing through the ice, hunting for polar bears, making igloos, and of life in a land where the days and nights were not like ours. The kindergartners learned that the hide of one large polar bear would make three pairs of pants for an Eskimo man. A large strip of paper was spread on the floor to give the children an idea of the size of one large polar bear. With much surprise they learned that a male polar bear has a *mane*. Eskimo ladies used this hair from the bear's mane to decorate their footwear. The Eskimo whose spear or gun first wounded the bear got to cut off the front one-third of the bear skin, to get the mane hair for his lady friend. The children thought that custom very fair! They spent some time measuring and cutting the top one-third of the simulated bear skin.

There were many class discussions about seal hunting, the trapping of foxes, walrus hunting and the preparation of fur. The children learned how husky dogs were harnessed to the sleds, how they were cared for, what they ate, how they kept warm at night by curling up beneath the snow, their warm breath helping to make an icy covering around them.

All this new knowledge about an unknown people was fascinating to these kindergartners. The globe was used to locate the arctic regions where Eskimos live, in Alaska and in Canada. When they learned that the name Eskimo means "eater of raw meat" they were quite unable to imagine the taste of it. They could not understand why an Eskimo child could love raw blubber as much as the kindergartners loved candy.

They used the word igloo freely, but were surprised to learn that it meant any kind of house made of blocks of snow, turf, animal skins, or stones. Construction projects of all kinds were in progress during the unit study on Eskimos. Icebergs made from papier-maché were painted, igloos were made from plaster of paris which was smoothed over paste-soaked paper on an oiled, upturned bowl, so that it would slide off easily when dry. The plaster was scored with a knife before it hardened, to resemble blocks of snow.

One child brought scraps of fur cloth and clothespins, from which Eskimo figures were fashioned. The children planned an Arctic scene, to be displayed on a table. They modeled sled dogs from clay but deemed them "too wobbly" to stand up under sled-pulling, so more dogs were made from balsa wood, with the children carving sled and dogs themselves. Match-stick legs were pegged into the wood with the teacher's help.

New vocabulary words had become common in the talk among the children as they worked. Igloo, kayak, umiak, mukluks, kamiks, harpoon, komatik were all names which the children used and which they could recognize in the story charts they had helped their teacher to make. They talked about the northern lights, how lamps were used for heat, light and limited cooking, that the fuel for the lamps was whale blubber or oil. They knew that Eskimo mothers carried their babies on their backs, next to their bodies, to keep them snugly warm. A pair of real Eskimo mukluks were inspected.

Many books about Eskimos were consulted and enjoyed at all times. The children began to recognize captions on pictures, as well as the same words on the charts they had helped to make.

To space-minded kindergartners, the round globe was a logical map on which to trace the travels of Eskimos as they searched for food. Baffin Island, the locality of several stories, was easily found. The globe study also involved the differences and likenesses between the north and south poles.

When a little boy asked, "I *know* how we could go to Alaska by plane and on the Alcan Highway, but how could we get there by boat?" the globe was again consulted as the trip was made from his Indiana school on Lake Michigan to the west coast, then by boat to Alaska.

Many language and number experiences were enjoyed by the kindergartners as they learned about Eskimos. An original song was a great favorite, and was also used as a finger play. Five tiny Eskimo figures were made from felt to fit over the fingers of teacher or student. They gave the song action and interest.

> Five little Eskimos in a row,
> Five little Eskimos in the snow.
> Along came a big white polar bear,
> And one little Eskimo scampered from there.
> (Four little Eskimos, etc.)

Using the same Eskimo pattern the teacher provided many felt and fur Eskimos, seals and fur polar bear figures for number games, which were played on the flannel board. After they had been introduced to the class, groups of children would play together with them, the natural leaders taking teaching roles. They did one-to-one matching, they "added to," "took away," arranged the figures in groups and used felt numerals to play number games.

The concept of thirds was easy to understand when paper, to simulate the bear hide, was put on the floor and *three pairs* of pants were cut from it. A circle was drawn on the floor to show how a snow-block igloo was constructed. A lively discussion of the way in which snow-blocks must be placed upward in *decreasing* amounts challenged the more alert thinkers. The yardstick was used to mark off on the floor the size of a dog sled.

Some children drew pictures of an Eskimo and made a game which they called, "How many fish should you put on Koweeka's line?" Numerals were displayed, one at a time. The player took the correct number of paper fish from a box and hung them on Koweeka's line with paper clips. That was a beloved game which every child wanted to play.

Finding rhyming words was a fascinating game. Seal, meal, sled, led, caribou, igloo, pack, kayak, umiak, bear, hair, foxes, boxes, snow, blow.

Who can say what limit there is to a kindergartner's ability to learn, his desire to project himself into the life and habits of a child in a part of the world so vastly different from his own? This particular learning experience began when a little boy brought something unusual to school to share and told his classmates about it. New and wonderful learning experiences *always* begin when young children may look, touch, listen, think about and question. Knowledge continues as the child participates in an exciting project which puts no boundaries on what he may learn, in the ways that are best suited to his abilities.

Indians

Children of all ages love to study about Indians, but kindergartners particularly enjoy the many activities that can be an integral part of learning about Indians. Many young children have seen real, twentieth century Indians, in Florida, in the western states, or in Canada perhaps, and these Indians have no resemblance to those they have seen on TV. They want to know why. When all their questions are answered in an interesting study of the Indian from the early days of the Pilgrims' first knowledge of him, through the Indian–white man relationship as our country was settled, young children have a new conception of the Indian, of his primitive culture.

They find role-playing and dramatizations enjoyable, and some Indian crafts are simple enough to be achieved by small fingers. Learning about Indians should be a flexible study (as all kindergarten studies are), for children in one group may want to learn all about the many types of Indian shelters in different parts of our country; others might be more interested in particular Indian tribes, or a study of all tribes; while another group would be interested in weapons for hunting and fighting, how they were made, and what the designs of them meant.

There is a wealth of reference material for children and teachers, whatever the interest of a group may be. This author used reference books without regard for age level, so long as the pictures in them were bright, clear and easily understood, for young children can acquire much knowledge from the study of good pictures and from discussions in class about them. Providing reference books on a table, always available to the children, is an excellent way to attain several learning goals: they find that books are a source of knowledge; they can learn by looking and discussing; pictures prompt questions and observations which provide the motivation for further research and discovery about the ways of people; when children find that their teacher cannot supply the information they need for some project, a book can often supply that information, and their search for it, with the help of their teacher, is a most rewarding experience.

Kindergartners enjoy Indian stories and rhythms. They like making their own drums and rattles, wristlets and anklets, which are made with bells, to wear during Indian dances. Indian masks and totem poles are fascinating to make, particularly when the children learn the significance of such designs as the thunderbird, the eagle, the fox and other objects found on Indian crafts.

Indian drum rhythms can be taught easily by showing children that knots are tied in a heavy string or leather thong at regular intervals to indicate the frequency of drum beats. Three knots tied in a string with short spaces then a long space, would indicate "Boom, Boom, Boom, Rest,—Boom, Boom, Boom, Rest." Soon the more musical children will be making up new rhythms and instructing their friends in the use of other knotted strings, which they have made to show the beat of the drums.

Masks can be constructed in a number of ways: as a drawing, on paper; by using paper bags, which can be worn over the head; on paper, aluminum or plastic plates; by using construction paper to make paper-sculptured masks. One method, which is not always a favorite with children, is to make a mask directly over the contours of a child's face. The child's features must be covered with oil or vaseline, then bands of paper toweling, slightly dampened with liquid starch, are applied directly to the child's face until he is thoroughly "bandaged." The mask then is very gently removed and allowed to dry. Painted, with yarn hair, the resulting Indian mask is truly the child's "own Indian face," but most kindergartners are reluctant to submit to the rather messy process involved in making such a mask.

Shields and bows and arrows can be made out of various materials. Children may want to construct an "adobe" house or pueblo out of boxes, one large enough to play in, or make tepees out of sheeting or heavy paper.

While learning about shelters, kindergartners become familiar with new words. Hogan, adobe, cliff-dwellings, long-houses, chikees (or chikis) are words which they understand, and learn to associate with the Indian tribes whose homes they are. Stories about Hopi Indians help kindergartners to understand the meaning of the word *mesa* and why the Hopi Indians built their homes on high mesas in the western United States. They learn why the Seminoles of Florida built their chikis on stilts and why most of the Seminoles no longer live in chikis.

Film strips (listed in the bibliography) are valuable teaching aids in showing children the Indians' early use of rafts, dug-out canoes and other primitive means of transportation. They show ancient customs of tribes and the way many Indians live today.

Math games were devised by the teacher with the help of the students. Pictures of tepees and Indians were made for a game of one-to-one matching. Numerals were employed for games which taught number concepts. (See Chapter 6 on Games.)

An Indian unit, which is developed from the varied interests of the kindergartners themselves, is an excellent way to reach learning goals for every child in the room, because whatever his intellectual ability, each child will find that the study of Indians will offer him activities commensurate with his ability.

Transportation

The ways people travel from place to place, the machines and methods used, both past and present, make the study of transportation exciting to every kindergartner. Air, land and water travel —one of these or all of these—will make a fascinating learning experience for children.

Dramatizations of train and plane rides, role-playing as captain of a ship, engineer of a train, pilot of a plane, all appeal to the young child. The opportunity to provide excellent learning experiences is limitless in a transportation unit. All areas for extending a child's comprehension of his world can be explored and all learning activities correlated in an engrossing study of the mobile life which most young children have experienced in one way or another before they enter school. If city children or those from culturally deprived homes have had no actual experience in travel, they can learn much from stories, discussions and dramatizations in the classroom.

A study of transportation can offer many diversified learning experiences, any or all of which can be used if the children show sustained interest. Wheels and machines, planes, gliders, rockets, space ships, trains (electric, steam or diesel-powered), boats, cars, trucks, buses, bicycles, motorcycles, scooters, animals that help people travel, all are topics of interest about which children might want to build a study unit.

The opportunity for acquiring new vocabulary words is an excellent one. Just learning the names and uses of cars which make up a freight train can be a valuable experience to the young child. Once he becomes familiar with train cars, an absorbing study can be made of products which are shipped in various kinds of cars to the town where the child lives. Which of these products does he require for daily living? An interesting bulletin board and map study can help a kindergartner to get a concept of his needs and the vast areas of his country which supplies those needs. Some articles are shipped from across the United States by train, plane or truck, he discovers, while some may come part of the way by water.

When learning about trains an interesting project is to set up a train of shoe boxes, each with a name like hopper, boxcar, refrigerator-car, tanker, etc. on it. Into these boxes children may put individually drawn pictures or magazine pictures of objects whose names begin with the letter and sound of c, h, b, t and so on. Kindergartners love this sort of game. The slower ones are helped to find pictures in magazines, or to make their own. Their more alert classmates patiently help them with their sounds.

Comparative distances are considered when the question is posed, "What kind of transportation would you use to go from your home in (any town) to (any town) in the quickest possible way?" If a child chooses air travel, then a lively discussion may develop, because the alert thinkers will decide that it would take longer to drive to an airport than to drive a car to a nearby destination. Another question that elicits contradictory answers is, "What would be the slowest method of transportation you use?" Children that are creative thinkers have a delightful time with such thought-provoking questions.

Stories of travel over the earth's surface help children to understand how difficult it has always been to build roads and railroads through mountainous areas. They begin to get some idea of the difficulty American pioneers had in traveling west. Geography and history enter into the study of transportation in a natural way as young children discuss and compare old and new ways of travel. Whatever their ability, all children find transportation an engrossing subject.

Citizenship

There are many ways in which the kindergarten teacher may help her children to become good citizens, at school, in their homes and in their community. (See Chapter 3.) When a child has learned to live cooperatively with his classmates, when he has learned to be responsible for his own behavior, he has made progress toward good citizenship. In presenting her learning program, his teacher will plan many activities to help each child in her room to identify them with his own experiences, and to become aware of his own needs so that he may also be concerned with the needs of others. Children's interests can create excellent opportunities for helping them to social growth. The study units presented here were all developed as the result of children's observations and desire to know more about themselves and their community.

Learning to Be a Good American Citizen

In a class discussion one day a kindergarten teacher discovered that twenty-four of her thirty-eight students had moved to their present homes, in the midwest, from other states. When two children began to question each other, "How close did you live to me when I lived in Baltimore and you lived in New Jersey?" she showed them a map of the United States. She explained that Baltimore was a *city* in Maryland, but New Jersey was a *state*. The attention of all the children in the group became centered on how to determine the distance between the city and the state. They asked innumerable questions about states and cities, naming those where grandparents lived, or those where they had formerly lived. They were intrigued by observing the distances on the map between their old and their new homes.

The large map the children consulted was part of the equipment in that kindergarten room. On it each state had been tinted, by the teacher, to exactly match their map-puzzle pieces. Many kindergartners had played with this map puzzle each day, matching the pieces to the larger tinted map on the wall, but it had been merely a puzzle, and they had attached no particular meaning to the relationship of the states to each other.

Suddenly the names and locations of states had a new meaning for these children. Now they began to identify themselves with the state that was their birthplace, and the state in which they now lived. A study unit began to grow, as the children's interests grew. The teacher projected a map of the United States on white

Figure 7.

paper, so that it covered an entire bulletin board. She enlisted the aid of the children who could trace the projected lines on the paper. This time she tinted only those states in which the kindergartners had formerly lived. They, too, were colored to match the map puzzle, for ease of identification. Their own midwest state was tinted, for some of the children had never lived in any other community. Each child in the room made a small likeness of himself and the figure was located in the state where he was born. The fourteen children who had been born in the local community were encouraged to be quite proud, because *they* were "natives" of their state. (A kindergarten teacher must always be sensitive to the needs of young children to feel equally important, equally loved.)

All but twelve of the children had moved to Indiana from *eastern* states. That brought up questions like these: Why had the fathers of these children moved to Indiana? What kinds of jobs did these fathers have that would send them from the eastern states to the mid-western states? Why were there so many factories in the east? Why was the eastern part of the United States settled before the western part? Why was it hard for people to travel to the west? How did they travel?

From an interesting and absorbing study of the early settlement of the United States the discussions led to many phases of its settlement, the life of pioneers in the eastern states, the hardships of pioneers who endured the long journey to the west. This brought in discussions about modes of transportation, mountains, rivers, deserts, prairies, Indian life. The study involved construction and art work. Some children brought in articles which had been used by early pioneers, and many stories were read which helped the kindergartners to get an idea of their forefathers' struggle to settle their country. Figure 7 shows a discussion of covered wagons in the kindergarten classroom.

Some pertinent facts were remembered by each child as he realized his heritage, and his place as a future citizen of a great country. This chart was made:

> We all live in Indiana.
> We all live in the United States.
> We all live in North America.

We all live on a continent.
We all live on the planet Earth.

The United States flag belonged to all of them, so they discussed in detail their need to always keep the flag clean; to keep the flag off the floor or the ground; to carry the flag on a pole or a staff; to remove hats (if a boy or man) when the flag is presented; to always love and respect the flag. Being citizens of the United States meant that grown-ups were able to vote. The kindergartners were interested in voting. Many knew what voting machines looked like. They were given the opportunity to participate in voting by secret ballot in their room, so they might have an idea of the procedure and the responsibility of making a choice of candidates. Two candidates were chosen by popular vote and their names were printed in large letters which every kindergartner could recognize. A voting booth was provided (a bulletin board and easel served very well to make an enclosure for privacy) and pieces of paper and a black crayon were put on a chair beside the box for the votes. As each child entered the booth he was instructed to print the name of his chosen candidate on a piece of paper, fold the paper and put it in the box. The children took the procedure very seriously and even the slower learners followed the directions exactly, printing their candidate's name with great care. It was an exciting experience in practical learning for future citizenship.

The learning opportunities in this study of citizenship were of great value to these young children. They do not retain all the information they acquire in such a study, but later, as they go into other grades, when similar facts are presented, they may say, "Oh, I remember, we talked about that once." Shared learning, which results from the interests of the children, is very meaningful and the carry-over into other areas of knowledge is great.

What Do the Signs Say?

Young children are very curious about signs on the streets, in the school building, in their kindergarten room. Many of them have learned what the traffic signs say, long before they come to school. In their room there are signs which they quickly learn

Figure 8.

Figure 9.

to recognize: GIRLS, BOYS, SCISSORS, PAPER, CHALK, VISITOR'S CHAIR, etc. A study of signs is an excellent way to acquaint kindergartners with signs which warn them of danger or help them to find their way around their own community. The book, *Let's Find Out What the Signs Say* is a help in teaching recognition and meanings of signs. (See bibliography.)

Every child in the room can contribute to a study project about signs. POISON, KEEP AWAY, DANGER and other signs concerned with safety are familiar to some children and they share their knowledge with the others. They may want to make charts, or individual booklets to take home, and do their own printing or art work on the projects. They may enjoy playing games which involve identification of signs. One game uses large cards with signs printed on them, KEEP OFF THE GRASS, FIRE, HELP, BOOKS, BUS STOP, GO, STOP, SCHOOL, DRIVE CAREFULLY, GAS, etc. It is helpful if traffic and road signs are made in exactly the proper shapes used on the highway. The signs are put upside down on a table and a child must turn them over, then repeat the names of all he can remember seeing there. Scores may be kept. This is an enjoyable game which children will play together at playtime. Variations of the game may have a child identify signs that begin with the first letter of his name, or signs whose names start with familiar sounds; another variation is to have children look at the signs and designate their uses, as in-the-house signs, schoolroom signs, signs that warn a child to "be careful," signs that give directions (as TURN RIGHT, TURN LEFT) and signs that are the names of things, like ZOO, SCHOOL, DRUG STORE. It is surprising to find that children can learn so much from a WHAT DO THE SIGNS SAY? project.

Don't Be a Litterbug

It was a windy Monday in spring and the school grounds were covered with debris when the kindergartners went out to play. Neighborhood children of all ages used the play equipment on weekends; milk cartons, pop bottles, candy wrappers, Popsicle sticks, broken glass and papers blown there by the wind made the play area an unsightly place.

The kindergartners complained about it. They were quite self-righteous in their indignation. "*We* don't throw things around like this! *We've* learned how to clean up the messes we make! The big kids should be ashamed!"

After playtime, back in their schoolroom a group of children brought up the subject of litter on the school playground and asked if they might make a "long picture with some writing on it," to put out in the hall. They thought the "big kids" would read it and, as one little girl put it, "be minded to pick up their stuff."

Everybody agreed that their older brothers and sisters in school told *them* what to do all the time, so maybe they should do a little telling. Their motives may have been those of self-righteous do-gooders but the project turned out to be an excellent one, in which each kindergartner took an active part.

The "long picture" was very good, and needed very little "writing" to get its message across. The children composed an original song and an original fingerplay which were written down by their teacher. They enjoyed these in their room, and a copy of the song was put up beside the picture, in a central hall where children of all grades could read it.

The message was extremely effective. The picture, captioned ARE *YOU* A LITTERBUG? attracted much attention for weeks. The kindergartners were very proud to have made a contribution which was noticed and acted upon by older boys and girls.

The fingerplay:

This little litterbug dropped his papers,
This little litterbug threw some sticks.
This little litterbug messed up his schoolyard,
This little litterbug broke some bricks.
This little litterbug was busy and sweet,
He picked up the litter to make everything neat.

The song, set to the tune of Yankee Doodle:

We don't like a litterbug,
He messes up his own school.
He throws his papers all around,
He disobeys the rules.

Chorus:

Litterbugs are naughty children,
Litterbugs are careless, too.
They never pick up things they drop,
They always spoil the view.

If you see a litterbug
In your school or on your street,
Tell him he must change his ways,
He must learn to be neat.

Safety

Every kindergarten teacher has her own ideas about how safety should be taught in the area where her school is located. City children who must cross busy streets need a different kind of instruction than country children who attend schools by bus. The need to adapt a study unit to her own group is true of every program the teacher plans, of course. Varied learning experiences are a part of the young child's life at home and at school, and the alert teacher is quick to capitalize on the eagerness children show about new projects and the excitement they feel when they have been a part of an enjoyable learning experience. It becomes more meaningful because it was *their* idea, they helped to develop it, each child had some part in making the activity a success.

Children's interests do not have to be of major importance to make worthwhile projects; but the learning which results from activities developed from those interests *is* truly significant. If the kindergarten teacher allows her children to experiment, to create, to feel pride in a project which is truly their own, if she gives them time to observe and discuss, to handle and manipulate, to investigate, to search out information for themselves, then she has made a major contribution to their intellectual development.

6

Creative Games
with
Specific
Learning Goals

As the kindergarten teacher helps her students develop study units from their interests, she will find ways to introduce many simple games that have definite learning goals and skills as their objectives. These "games-that-teach" are very effective when they are correlated with activities which have been chosen and planned by the kindergartners.

The games mentioned in this chapter cannot begin to touch on all the limitless areas of learning in the kindergarten; they may be used as presented here; they may be adapted to the particular needs of specific groups of kindergartners; they may suggest ways in which to devise games for teaching skills which have not been mentioned here.

Materials needed for most "games-that-teach" are simple and inexpensive. Felt pieces in attractive colors may be purchased in most dime stores, and the teacher who cannot draw her own designs, for numerals and countless objects which she may want to make from felt, can always use patterns. A large felt board is a necessary piece of kindergarten equipment. Some teachers also provide five or more smaller felt boards for children to use while playing games together in groups.

Geometric figures made from cardboard, felt or colored paper are needed. Many teachers make sure that the kindergarten room has calendars, globes, maps, parquetry puzzles, magnetized boards with magnetized letters and numerals, wooden or plastic objects which show halves, thirds and fourths, blocks of geometric shapes, rulers, measures for liquids, a thermometer, a simple scale or balance, a displayed alphabet. Such standard equipment can be supplemented by objects made from cloth and cardboard, or from materials furnished by children. Miniature toys, plastic spoons, etc., can be used for counting games. An ingenious teacher will substitute available materials for those she does not have, and devise many challenging games to hold the interest of her kindergartners.

Games to Develop Listening Skills and Increase Attention Spans

At the beginning of the school year, when the attention of five-year-olds tends to wander, their teacher can play various "listening" games with them to help them to increase their attention spans and to develop their listening skills.

She may choose a story which proves to be a universal favorite, then read it frequently until she makes sure that every word in the story is familiar to the children in the room; then she may first read the story and miscall a name, observing the children's reaction to her "mistake." Gradually she will change whole paragraphs or the sequence of happenings. When the kindergartners become alerted to her challenge of their listening, they delight in the game, and she can use variations of the procedure in other learning areas where listening and alertness for detail are essential.

Many number rhymes, such as "One, two, button my shoe" can be used in a similar way to make children alert to number concepts. The same rhymes can be used by first providing the children with paper and crayons; then when the teacher's voice abruptly stops, the children are asked to make as many circles (or other objects) on their papers as the last number they heard her mention.

Another similar game, played with paper and crayons, is to name familiar stories or poems whose titles contain numbers of things, as in *The Three Billy Goats Gruff, The Seven Diving Ducks, Three Little Pigs, The Three Bears, Ten Little Indians, Ciceley G. and the Nine Monkeys,* etc. When the teacher's voice pauses, the children make marks on their papers to show the number last heard.

To teach listening and following-directions skills, papers may be provided on which a circle, square, triangle and rectangle appear. (This, of course, after children have learned to recognize these shapes.) Then specific directions can be given to make two kites *inside* the circle, four balls *outside* the square, three circles inside the *triangle,* five apples in the *rectangle.* Children love this sort of game. Some need to ask a neighbor to repeat the directions, because they cannot concentrate enough to remember them, but most kindergartners take pride in following detailed directions, and they listen intently.

Another game to lengthen attention spans is a simple "talking" game, played with the children in a circle. Some familiar word, like *fall* is casually introduced as "The time of year. Can you think of another way we use the word fall?" Somebody suggests, *hurting yourself, mama's hairpiece,* or, rarely, a water-fall.

A question may be asked: "How can we talk about time?" Children may reply that time can be a *minute,* a *second,* a *year,* a *week, forever,* a *jiffy, sometime, never, once upon a time, hardly ever.*

Amounts of things may be called a *piece,* a *number-like-three, none, not enough, every bit,* a *speck,* a *smidgen,* etc.

A discussion of coats could bring out names like *wraps, capes, shawls, stoles;* and the number and variety of words in such games tend to disclose the economic and cultural background of the individual kindergartners. Children who have traveled, or who have heard many stories at home, may suggest names like *serape* or *parka.* Such terms, which are unfamiliar to most of the members of the group, may spark a lively, informative discussion of the people who wear such coats; may even serve to intrigue the children's interest so that a unit of study results.

A discussion of head coverings may serve the same purpose; or one of foot coverings, which might bring out such terms as *clogs, moccasins, brogans, mukluks,* etc. Children from foreign homes often make interesting contributions in such discussions and benefit from their classmates' attention and interest.

Spatial relationships and distances are fun to talk about in this way, as *inside, on, under, above, beneath, outside, around, beyond, over there, a little ways, nearby, close to,* etc.

Colloquialisms or comparisons sometimes enter into discussions of things that belong together, like *twins, pairs, dozens, nest full, families, flocks, herds, clutch, a mess of, a swarm.* Children enjoy hearing new names for familiar things; they like to talk about words that sound the same or are the same word, words that rhyme; they like to have a try at coining their own words. Such discussions stimulate creative thinking and presently even the slow-thinkers are making contributions.

Games in Following Directions

Games for listening and following directions somewhat overlap each other, as a child must *listen* and then *act* in correct sequential order to play such games. The games suggested here are to help children to concentrate on doing exactly what has been asked of them, and to carry out a task in the way it should be done. Experiences of this sort prepare a child to listen carefully and to understand directions given to him when he reaches first grade.

A basic game: The teacher directs a child to touch his chair, touch her desk, touch the piano and return to his chair, increasing the number of objects to be touched in *exact sequence* by one each time around until the child is touching from six to eight objects. A variation to teach math terms and number concepts is to ask Susan to run around the table three times, then ask Mark to run around the table *two more* times than Susan; Mary runs three *less* times than Mark, etc. At the end of the game a lively discussion may develop about which child ran *more* times, *fewer* times, the *same amount of times,* etc.

One child may be instructed to put a pencil on the piano bench, a marble in the box, a chair in the corner, while the directions immediately following, for another child, tell him to put the pencil in the *box* and then place box and chair behind the desk. This game and its variations require listening and concentration, as well as the ability to accurately follow the given directions. It involves every-member participation, for the other listening kindergartners are always eager to catch a classmate in a mistake.

Children like this game, too: "Look at Susan. Touch all the *pairs* of things you see on Susan." (Eyes, ears, hands, feet, shoes, socks, arms, legs, nostrils, hair-barrettes or ribbons, rings, etc.) It may be varied to include "threes" or "fives" in the classroom, "stacks of," "dozens of," all of which are excellent devices for helping even the slow learners to acquire knowledge of terms, to make counting and grouping meaningful, and to have a clear concept of ways in which objects may be associated with each other.

Games to Teach Number Concepts

When young children first enter school they need to play many games which will involve simple counting, and may want to help make nonsense rhymes, "One, two, these games are new. Three, four, touch the floor. Five, six, boys and girls mix. Seven, eight, jump over the gate. Nine, ten, do it again," patterned after the old rhyme, "One, two, button my shoe." Another rhyme can be started, "One, two, three, Take a walk with me. Four, five, six, We'll find some sticks. Seven, eight, nine, These stones are mine (or, Turn at the sign, etc.)." Kindergartners are very enthusiastic about games of this sort and very helpful in suggesting words which fit into the rhymes.

Meaningful counting may be started from the beginning of school when taking attendance, by counting the number of girls, the number of boys, and the total number of children present. Absences may be discussed at first, and questions asked, "Is today's attendance *greater than* or *less than* yesterday's attendance? Are there more girls here today than yesterday?" If the attendance is put up on the chalk board and asterisks are given for perfect attendance, they will furnish additional opportunities for learning number concepts. The kindergartners will enjoy counting the stars. They can make comparisons about whether the number of asterisks the boys have is *greater than* or *less than* those which the girls have. They can decide how many *more* stars one group must have to catch up with the other group. If the numerals, which represent the daily attendances of girl and boy groups, and for the total attendance, are kept on the board, the children will begin to recognize numerals beyond 10 and some of them will be able to tell their teacher how to write 16 or 19, or 23 perhaps. This is an enjoyable game and one in which even the slower students may participate.

A teacher can make excellent use of felt objects and felt numerals when giving instruction in the terms *numeral* and *number*. Felt animals and objects can be used to make sets, in joining these sets to make new sums, in re-naming the numerals 2, 3, 4, 5, etc.; for equivalent sets, and one-to-one matching.

The felt board, with numerals and rows of matching objects, can be used for teaching ordinals. There are also many rhymes and fingerplays which teach ordinals. Seasonal ones, such as this, are a great favorite:

> Five big turkeys perched on a gate.
> The first one said, "It's getting late."
> The second one asked, "Do you see a man?"
> The third one said, "Yes! With a roasting pan!"
> The fourth one gobbled, "Let's run very fast!"
> The fifth one said, "Until Thanksgiving's past!"
> They talked it over and agreed they were right.
> Away through the air
> They all took flight.

When units of social study are being taught, objects can be cut from felt and used to correlate number concepts with newly acquired knowledge of other people and their ways. It is fun for kindergartners to arrange equivalent sets, to do one-to-one matching when the objects they use are snowmen figures and hats, or brooms, mittens, etc. They like to put cowboys on horses, Indians into canoes or tepees; Eskimos can hunt for seals or polar bears, boy and girl figures can engage in many interesting and meaningful activities while number games are played.

Colored felt bird shapes can be used in games children will play in a group with their teacher, or at play time with each other. "There are six bluebirds on the telephone wire. Three flew away. How many are left?" "I want to see seven bluebirds on the wire. How many must fly back?" This kind of play can involve many variations of the game and allow each child in the group to play.

Their teacher will introduce many games to show kindergartners how to rename the numerals 2–10, and will direct many discussions about them. These rhyming games, used with a felt board, felt objects and numerals are fun to play.

To rename 5:

>Five little puppies were playing with each other.
>2 brown puppies said, "Let's go find our mother."
>2 black puppies looked for some bones.
>1 white puppy was left all alone.

To rename 6:

>Six little birds perched in a tree.
>1 yellow bird sang, "Listen to me!"
>3 red birds decided to fly.
>2 birds were left, as blue as the sky.

To rename 7:

>Seven ducks had feathers of yellow.
>4 ducks said, "We are fine fellows."
>1 duck went to the pond for a swim.
>2 ducks that were left said, "Look at him!"

To rename 8:

>Eight little bells hung on a string.
>5 blue bells began to ring.
>2 red bells fell to the ground.
>1 gold bell whirled round and round.

To rename 9:

>Nine white rabbits were sitting on a hill.
>4 bunnies sat very still.
>2 of them hopped away.
>3 together began to play.

Children will find it amusing to make up their own rhymes to rename numerals. They may suggest number games, or variations of those which are suggested by their teacher. Activities prompted by their own interests are very meaningful to kindergartners.

Games which involve a young child's mental and physical participation are excellent learning devices and many will be discussed later in this chapter. Two such games, which teach number concepts, are presented here. The first one is a dismissal game. A large calendar is used, with large black numerals. The teacher can explain about some months having 30 days, while others have 31 days, and February is in a class by itself. The game (and calendar) will have as many days shown as the school month in which it is played. A card is given to each child, on which a numeral from 1 to 30 (or 31) is printed. As the numerals representing the days of the month are called, and pointed to by the teacher, the child holding the matching numeral must present his card, before going to get his coat for dismissal. When the game has been played a few times, many children in the class will recognize not only the numeral on their own cards but those numerals on cards held by children around them. Any child failing to recognize the numeral he holds is helped to find its match on the calendar. After this game has been played many times, the teacher may merely point to the numeral on the calendar and the child must call its name before he is excused. This teaches recognition of numerals beyond 10, by name as well as by sight.

A physical activity game, which is used for exercise and relaxation, can also be varied to teach number concepts. It is the old standby, *Little Brown and White Ponies,* which is familiar to all kindergarten teachers. When the game is introduced the yardstick is examined, the markings on it are discussed and the children begin to get an idea of measurement. An inch is a measure of length, and it will always be the same. There are 36 of these inches on a yardstick, and there are numerals there, from 1 to 36. The yardstick is used to measure many familiar objects in the room, until the kindergartners begin to understand its use, and the new and interesting things measurement can tell them. A "gate" is started with one block, 3″ x 2″ x 12″, and the gate is made taller by the addition of one block at a time as the game progresses. Each child in the *White Ponies* group and each child in the *Brown Ponies* group is given the opportunity to jump the gate at each new level. Any child who kicks the gate down as he attempts to jump over is asked to sit down. As each new block is added the distance, from its top to the floor, is measured. A few children can jump over a "gate" 21 inches high but the average kindergartner takes pride in jumping a 12″ gate, or one 15 inches high. Children vie with each other for the privilege of measuring with the yardstick. As a result of this activity kindergartners often use the yardstick to measure other objects in the room, both horizontally and vertically, with interesting results.

Games to Teach Perception of Sounds

Young children are fascinated by sounds. They love to hear them and they love to make them. When they enter kindergarten they have learned to make many sounds which they associate with objects. They have learned that pictures have names, and at the beginning of school each child is helped to recognize certain combinations of letters which his teacher tells him are the *picture* of his own name, and those letters also make the *sound* of his name. He already knows the sound of his name, now he has learned how his name looks. The *picture* of his name may be found on many things in the room. A name card or tag may hang on a string around his neck, or be pinned to his coat. His name may appear on a big paper on the wall, along with other printed letters, which represent the pictures and sounds of his friends' names.

Most children learn to recognize their printed names quickly if they are allowed to play games which involve their names. Kindergartners may sit in a circle, each child holding a card on which his printed name appears. As the teacher holds up a duplicate card and a child realizes that it matches the card he holds, he may turn a somersault in the middle of the circle, or perform some physical feat as his reward. Recognition of name cards may also be used in sending children from the circle to play tables; or as a means to give turns for getting milk. The teacher will devise many ways to familiarize children with their own names and the names of their classmates. The *Name Game,* as kindergartners call it, is a great favorite, and will be requested long after the children have become quite familiar with the sound and sight of their own names.

Once children have become familiar with the sight of their names, they are ready to learn the sounds with which their names begin. An alphabet needs to be prominently displayed in the kindergarten room for this and many other interesting "sounds" games. Children quickly learn that each pictured letter of the alphabet says its own name and has at the very least one other sound. (All that needs to be learned at this point is the short vowel sound, a soft g, etc.) A child, Tommy, may find the letter T, and knows it says *tee* but also *tuh,* which is the way his name starts. Amy and Alice each recognize the letter A, they know that A says its own name, as in Amy, but it has another sound when it says the A in Alice. When the teacher begins to call out the sounds of the alphabet, Alex, Andrew, Amy and Alice may go to get their coats (or start some other activity). Bobby, Belinda, Bruno and Benny may go next. When the game is first introduced, a few children need to be helped by their classmates. Soon each child knows not only the sound which begins his own name, but recognizes all, or nearly all, of the other beginning sounds as well, and can point out the letters which make the sounds.

Other sound games may be played while kindergartners sit in a circle. They may think of toys whose names begin with a suggested sound, or pick out objects in the room, and ask each other to point to the alphabet letter whose sound begins the name of the object. Their teacher may want to discuss with them the "feel" of sounds in their mouths, the mechanics of using tongue and lips to make sounds. Young children delight in this kind of game, for they have loved making sounds from an early age when they began first to babble, then to hum, croon and sing, and to imitate motor sounds in play. Games make words and sounds meaningful to the child as he uses his senses to *hear* sounds, to *feel* their shapes in his mouth, to *see* the shapes of the letters which represent sounds. Later he may *touch* cardboard or felt letters or use his finger to trace letters which name sounds; or he learns to make them on paper.

Games to Teach Recognition of Letters

Many of the games mentioned in the discussion of sounds are excellent to use in teaching recognition of letters, as in the "Name Game." Small objects may be displayed on a table; then a familiar letter, B perhaps, is held up. "John," his teacher may ask, "how does this letter say its name? Can you find objects on this table whose names start with B?" When John has found a ball, Band-Aid, box, bottle and a bead, his teacher then shows him a list of words. "Do you see any names here that start with the letter B?" John finds them easily and asks his teacher to tell him what the words say. Some words may name objects which are not displayed on the table. Kindergartners like this game and often request that pictures of the objects accompany the word lists, so they may learn to match word and picture. When playing this game together they may spell the words aloud together. This advanced activity appeals to the bright child, and perhaps to the average child, and the slow learner often picks up a surprising amount of knowledge from watching and listening to the others.

Large cardboard letters placed around the room can designate something exciting like a cave. At a given signal each kindergartner must run to the "cave" whose letter is the same as the beginning letter of his name.

A boy and girl leader may choose sides, and the contestants line up, facing each other. Each child is given a large letter. Beginning with the leader, each player must take his turn, name his letter and think of a word which begins with his letter. A child who fails to name his letter correctly must sit down until the end of the game. The side with the most children standing (correct answers) wins, of course; then those children who did not recognize their letters are helped to identify them.

At the beginning of school a "leader" holder may be displayed, on a level easily reached by the kindergartners. This holder can be a simple device, made of oaktag and bound on the edges with colored tape. It has two pockets, marked BOY LEADER and

GIRL LEADER, which hold the children's name cards. The children serve as leaders in rotation, two new leaders every day. As the "leader holder" is within reach, the children can constantly check their names. Soon they will learn to recognize the letters in their own names and many names belonging to their friends. Kindergartners who use this device are often overheard saying, "Ten more days before I'm the leader, Billy. You'll be leader two days after me." Two children may inform their teacher, "We'll be the leaders in three more days." Her reply might be, "How nice that you each can be a leader this week"; to which they may answer, "Not *this* week! You said we have only two more school days this week. *Next* week we'll be leaders." Some children may have advanced so far in their thinking that they will designate the *first* day of next week as their day to share leadership. Such a device as the "leader holder" not only encourages the children in sound and letter recognition, but stimulates them to think in comparative numbers, *befores, afters, days-this-week, the first day next week*. Because a child relates each thinking process to himself, as he anticipates the satisfaction of being a leader, he is eager to search for the information he wants.

Many kindergarten teachers find magnetized letters and boards are excellent teaching aids in their room. A file box of cards may be provided for each board. On each card is a picture and the name of the object shown. Children enjoy working in groups and "spelling" with magnetized letters the words on the cards, which they know, because of the accompanying pictures, to be house, mouse, boy, dog, boat, etc. At activity time children may want to compete with each other. Some remarks overheard at activity time are, "Look, MOUSE takes the same letters as HOUSE only the M is different." "I need some e's. You've got two e's in TREE and I need two in BEE." "We're making H words today." "Then we're taking the *at* words." "There's not any *at* words." "There is, too, stupid." Here picture cards are presented as proof. "See? There's C AT and H AT and R AT," and the child, satisfied to have made her point, lined up her *at* words on her magnetized board.

Games to Involve the Child Both
Mentally and Physically

Many of the games-that-teach, which have already been presented elsewhere in this chapter, involve the kindergarten child's mental and physical participation.

A game to familiarize children with the terms *first, next, last, middle, center,* may be played by lining children up in ascending or descending order, then asking someone to find the *middle* child in the line, the *next-to-the-last,* the child *behind* Robert, the *fourth* child *from* Jerry who heads the line; the teacher may want someone to tell her who is between Tommy and Helen. Physical activity may then be introduced, when the children understand the terms being used. The *third from the last* child may run to the head of the line, the *middle* child in the first line may exchange places with the *last* child in the second line, and so on. This sort of game instructs and interests; the children must be alert as it offers mental and physical activity.

A talk-about-and-do game begins with a story, "It Looks Like This" by Irma E. Webber, and becomes first a discussion, then a demonstration by children. It concerns the shapes of objects, and how they seem to change when they are viewed from different angles. Toys in the room are examined and viewed from various angles. Two children lie sideways, two stand facing the group, two stand with their backs to the group, two lie feet first, two lie head first on the floor, while the others in the group view them critically. Kindergartners have many comments to make about this activity. It challenges their thinking and many of them want to create pictures of animals or people, showing how they look when viewed from different angles.

Another talk-about-and-do game starts with a lively discussion of the sizes of things and the relationships of objects to each other. "What do we mean when we say something is tall?" the teacher asks. (Short? Wide? Narrow?) She points out that a fly is big when he sits beside an ant. Is a fly big when he sits on a giraffe? The giraffe is a large, tall animal when he stands beside a little boy. Is the giraffe a large, tall animal when he stands beside a city sky-scraper? Children will want to compare the sizes of things in their room at home; for example, their toys. This discussion opens up ways to experiment with materials. A piece of elastic is short, but it can be stretched to become long. An inflated balloon is large, but it becomes very small when the air escapes. A little girl is small, but her own shadow is tall. Books to read, before or after a game like this one, are *The Size of It* by Ethel S. Berkley and *The Giant Story* by Beatrice Schenk de Regniers.

Puppets may be used in the above games, and children will probably offer many good suggestions about how to make them. By manipulating puppets they learn about uniformity and perspective, differences and likenesses. They are surprised to learn that an object does not always look the same to two people who view it from exactly the same angle; that what we see depends upon many things besides the actual shape of the object before us. Kindergartners learn to do critical thinking in an activity of this kind.

Role-playing is always an effective way to catch the interest of a young child, and the alert teacher will use dramatizations whenever possible to make learning a meaningful, pleasant experience for her kindergartners. Learning to tell time may be dramatized, with children taking the parts of the hands and the numerals. The clock face can be sketched with chalk on the floor or made from large pieces of paper, taped together. A dramatization can be used to teach the use of the ruler and yardstick, too, and children will contribute good ideas about this role-playing.

Old favorite games like Squirrel in the Tree or an adapted version called Indians in the Tepees can be excellent math games as well as delightful physical activities. If two children make one tree, and three children make one tepee, and six trees (or tepees) are needed, how many children all together will be needed? If eight squirrels (or Indians) are playing, how many, at a given signal, can find a tree (or tepee) if only one squirrel is allowed to a tree? How many squirrels will be left out in the cold each time? If the number of trees or tepees is constantly changed, as well as the number of squirrels or Indians, and the kindergartners are allowed to do the figuring, these games become excellent learning experiences.

Games which involve a child's mental and physical participation in the same activity can be devised from most learning experiences. As one kindergartner remarked, "It's fun to learn new stuff because I use all of me to learn with."

7

Solutions for
Problems
of
Disruptive Behavior

Problems of misbehavior in the kindergarten classroom constantly interfere with the teacher's objectives for her children, as she plans learning and achievement goals in various areas of interest. It is not uncommon to have the disruptive behavior of one child completely spoil an interesting project or experiment in which all the children are engaged. His behavior distracts and annoys them and spoils their enjoyment of the activity. They resent his demands on the teacher's attention and their hostility only makes him more ingenious in devising ways to disturb the group. The child who is guilty of deliberate or conscious misbehavior is a child who needs help. There may be many reasons for his conduct and it is a fortunate teacher who finds a child's problems are simple ones which she can easily solve. Too often the problems that cause disruptive behavior are not immediately apparent to the teacher, but are obscurely buried in the child's emotional or social background. They may have their origin in home or parental influences; in some deep-seated, imperative need which impels the child to seek attention by disruptive behavior.

The teacher should recognize certain behaviors as red flags to warn of dangerous adjustment patterns; she should seek and find ways to help the disturbed child resolve his difficulties.

Children with Emotional and Social Disturbances

It is the kindergarten teacher's desire and obligation to find reasons for a child's disruptive behavior, when possible; to answer the desperate appeal he is making for help, for sometimes that is exactly what his actions are. She wants to help him adjust to his group and find acceptance, which he so obviously needs. When she has found the underlying reasons why a particular child behaves in an unacceptable manner, together they can establish new patterns of behavior. The child can become a real pleasure and asset in the room, a helpful member of his group. The teacher may find, as she studies the reasons for a child's misbehavior, that her *own* attitude toward that child must change before he can respond to her.

The many anecdotes and case histories in this chapter will show ways in which problems of misbehavior were investigated and solved.

The first one is about Toby, a little boy with a grave emotional problem. His teacher was aware that excessively quiet, withdrawn children often have pressures inside them that may become stronger than the controls they have set up against them. Such children sometimes have a violence potential. Because they are so unobtrusive and demand no attention from anyone, such children may go unnoticed; thus their troubles are harder to detect, harder to help.

From the first day of school Toby would not speak to the other children and always played alone. He spent his time under the table or under his chair, in his own quiet, lonely little world. Children in the room tried to draw him into their games, to help him to be a member of their group. His response was usually passively resistant, although sometimes he would strike out at them viciously and hurt some friendly child. He sometimes conformed enough to sit in the circle of children for discussions or stories, but he never spoke and refused to participate in any physical activity. His creative art was always the same composition, heavy concentrated color, in crayon or paint, black and sometimes purple. These compositions seemed to give him pleasure. He treasured them and took them home. The only time he made any sounds at all was when someone touched his pictures, or teased and threatened to tear them. Then he showed a fierce possessiveness toward what he had made.

His teacher, after observing him for several weeks, and giving him time to adjust to the group, called his mother and asked for a conference. When she came, Toby's mother was young and pretty, but a girl who was deeply, emotionally troubled. She talked freely about her own problems, which had started before college. She had married, at eighteen, an older man of whom she was obviously terrified. Crowds frightened her; she could not bring herself to shop in a crowded supermarket. She confessed to many personal fears.

Her attitude toward Toby was one of bewildered but genuine concern. His older brother was eight, a cruel child who loved to torment animals. He tormented Toby, too, dominating him completely in the home, destroying his toys, forcing him to participate in his strange activities. She admitted that she was unable to cope with her oldest son's behavior. The father traveled and was rarely at home. When she consulted him about the boys he was scornful of her anxieties, laughed at them and insisted that his older son was behaving exactly as *he* had behaved as a boy. When she tried to defend Toby, his father called him a "dumb kid" and a "scared rabbit" like his mother.

Toby's teacher made an appointment to visit him in his home. One afternoon, when she told Toby she would accompany him to his home, his eyes sparkled for an instant. "I will show you something," he told her.

He talked about how far it was to his house and about a pretty stone he had found in the road. The moment they reached his home Toby became very quiet, his friendliness gone. He hid himself behind a chair and listened as she talked to his mother. His brother came in noisily, then went out again. After an hour, when his teacher's efforts to communicate with Toby had failed, she remarked that she must go home. He emerged from his hiding place and said abruptly, "Wait." In a few moments he came back to her, in his hands a small truck and some little rubber animals. He talked about the animals.

"He hides his things," his mother explained, "because his brother tears them up when he thinks Toby likes them."

Before she left his home that afternoon, Toby's teacher and his mother made some plans. The older brother would go to school with other children in the neighborhood. Toby would leave much later, and bring some of his beloved toys to school to show his classmates. Toby agreed that he *might* share the things that interested him if the kids wouldn't touch them.

From this small start toward help and understanding for a little boy's problems, from these gestures of sharing, in a receptive atmosphere, with friendly and interested children, came a release to some of Toby's tensions, fears, and resentments. He learned to tell his classmates about the things he brought to school to show; of his own accord he abandoned his refuge under the table and sat in his chair. Shyly he joined in a few group activities. His creative pictures reflected his new acceptance of himself, and the friendship of his classmates, in the bright colors he used. Toby's mother reported that he was using his new-found confidence to resist his brother's cruelty, not with physical resistance but with an inner calm acceptance of his problem and his own ability to cope with it.

Margot was a loud and boisterous little girl, whose problem was a social one. She was a disturbing influence in the group, constantly interrupting to voice her opinions, dictating to her companions, hitting and shoving when they resisted her. She was a large child, who had a driving need always to be first, to sing louder than the others, to make the most elaborate pictures, to participate more violently in physical activities than anyone else. Her classmates disliked her and refused to play with her, which only intensified Margot's determination to be their leader.

She needed self-confidence and approval. She wanted desperately to be accepted by her classmates. Margot was too young to realize that constantly forcing herself on them made them reject her. Her teacher recognized her insecurity and had many talks with her. She was an intelligent child and finally understood that quiet helpfulness, real interest in other children's activities and a pleasant attitude toward her classmates could earn her the acceptance she wanted and needed. Margot gradually became a very sweet little girl, well liked and cooperative.

Emotional hungers can be as overpowering as physical hunger. Emotional needs are rooted deep within the individual. A young child does not know what is troubling him, cannot explain it, does not know that his misery is caused from tensions building up inside of him. Emotional problems, which manifest themselves in disruptive behavior, can be real barriers to learning. They challenge the teacher's concern and her desire to help the disturbed child.

On the first day of school a large man and a little boy entered the kindergarten room long before the other children were due to arrive.

The man gave the child a shove toward the teacher. "Here's another kid for you," he said. "He's a bad one, too. You've got my permission to beat him if he gets out of hand. That's what I do. I blister his bottom for him."

The teacher talked quietly with the man but realized at once that her questions must be carefully chosen for his answers were loud and cruelly truthful. The child listened to every word, but only shrugged when she spoke directly to him.

"*My* name's Brown, but his ain't. He's not my kid. My wife had him when she was in high school and I never even knew he existed till we'd been married two months. That was a lousy thing to spring on a man, and he's a lousy kid," the man confided, glaring at the little boy, who stared back. "Him and me don't hit it off. I don't want him, and his mother don't want him, neither, but when I raise a stink about him she says he's got nowhere else to go. So he stays. His name's Harry."

The man went away, the other new kindergartners arrived, and the child Harry quietly watched but said little, did not play with the children, and showed no enthusiasm for any activity. Poor little boy, thought his teacher, that dreadful man has taken all the spirit out of him.

She was wrong. During the first four weeks of school Harry showed exuberant spirits and was in constant trouble. He was mischievous, defiant, completely fearless, with no respect for his teacher and no consideration for the rights of other children. When he left a group of kindergartners they were always angry or weeping. His teacher had many talks with him. He was a bright child, with a very mature understanding of the adult motives in his world. "Everybody says I'm a bad kid, so I'll *be* a bad kid," he told his teacher. "Nobody likes me and I don't like nobody."

He resented her efforts to help him win the approval of his group. She knew he needed friendship desperately. He seemed suspicious of any person who was nice to him and for a time reacted to kindness with worse behavior than ever. He was compelled to be as trying as possible to prove that this kindness was genuine and not to be withdrawn just when he began to trust adults.

His teacher gave him many opportunities to show good leadership. Sometimes he failed her expectations, but now and then he showed her that beneath the hurt, defiant, disillusioned little boy was a fine child who needed status with his classmates, who had never before been important to anyone, who desperately wanted to be rewarded for some simple deed.

As he was drawn into class participation and planning of activities, the children discovered that Harry had good ideas, he knew how to play a lot of exciting games, he was fun to be with. They consulted him about how to build a space ship out of blocks, how to make a snow fort. There was no longer a need for Harry to brag and bully, for now he was accepted, he was a "good guy."

During the year there were many days when Harry came to school sullen and full of tensions. Sometimes he brought a note from home that bluntly and explicitly reminded his teacher, "You may think you've done a lot with this kid at school, but he's the same . . . kid at home he always was." Conferences with his parents were almost useless. His mother resented him because he was a constant reminder of a schoolgirl mistake and the chief reason she fought with her husband. His stepfather hated him for many reasons. On those days when things were bad at home, Harry's teacher demanded nothing of him until he was ready to join in the activities. He knew he was loved at school and that his participation was valued. When his courage and self-esteem were renewed by the warm acceptance of his teacher and classmates, Harry could once more become a valued, contributing member of his group.

Those problems of behavior which are caused by social maladjustment are easier to detect, manifesting themselves in aggressive, unacceptable behavior, as in the case of Margot. The child whose emotional disturbance is evidenced by withdrawal, as Toby's was, may not cause the immediate concern that the objectionably disruptive behavior causes, for his conduct is not actively disturbing to his teacher or his classmates. They may wonder why he behaves so strangely, but they are not personally affected by his withdrawal.

Children who are preoccupied with daydreams, or those who consistently feign illness or cry incessantly, are not happy, well-adjusted children. Their behavior is not that of mentally healthy children. Social and emotional problems that result in withdrawal or in recessive behavior may not be disruptive in the classroom, but the concerned kindergarten teacher will detect it and attempt to help the child to find a solution to his problems.

Home Difficulties, Parental Influences

Difficulties experienced in a child's home environment, parental influences and pressures, often cause disruptive behavior in the classroom. This is particularly true on the kindergarten level, for the child is too young to understand the reasons for the unhappy conditions in his home. He is too young to make the judgments which an older child might make to maintain emotional stability. The kindergartner only knows the misery and insecurity of a broken home where the father is absent and the whole atmosphere surrounding him is one of hate and rejection. Often severe poverty makes the problem even more difficult for the family, and all this is reflected in the child as rebellion and disruptive behavior.

Wally was brought to school on the first day by a neighbor. "His mother couldn't come," she explained to the kindergarten teacher. "She works. His dad ain't home. Him and her are sepa rated but he hangs around and it's bad for Wally. He stays with a baby-sitter, but she ain't too bright and he won't mind her He's a mean little kid. You'll have trouble with him. Good luck You'll need it!" All this was said in Wally's presence while he looked blankly into space, apparently unaware of the teacher and the other children in the room.

Wally was a naughty little boy, with a short attention span It seemed impossible for him to sit still to listen to a story, or to do creative work of any kind. He constantly annoyed his classmates by hitting, kicking, pinching them when they were playing or engaged in quiet activities. He boasted that he had an older brother. "He's a real mean kid and carries a knife! And he can use it, too!" Wally admired his brother.

The child revealed a deep resentment toward his mother be cause she was never at home. He pretended to hate his father too, but his teacher always knew when his father paid a visit to the home. While the visit lasted Wally was exhilarated at school and more disobedient than ever.

Attempts to have a conference with his mother failed. She protested that she did not have time, and seemed indifferent to Wally's problems. She informed the teacher that making the kid behave was *her* problem because, as his teacher, she was being paid to make him "toe the mark."

With no cooperation from Wally's parents, the teacher began her own rehabilitation program. He needed to acquire a feeling of being valued as a member of his group, instead of being dis liked because he was a torment and a tease. He was intelligent, and she began to challenge his thinking in many ways. She al ways praised him when he made a valuable contribution or a worthwhile suggestion. He was involved in activities that inter ested him and was so busy that he had no time to annoy his classmates. His teacher gave Wally responsibilities and soon dis covered that he had a great potential for leadership. When he realized that accepting responsibility gave him pleasure, and was valued by adults, he asked to run errands. The gradual change in his self-confidence and his newly acquired concept of himself as a helpful individual gave Wally a different sense of values

He no longer regarded his brother as an object of worship, confiding that he *knew* his brother did bad things. He was still affected by the unrest and quarreling in his home, but he did not revert to unacceptable behavior. Wally had found out *who* he was and *what* he was. He was important to other people. He became a diligent worker in the room and his help was always available when other children needed it.

Allie, Morton and Emil all had problems resulting from parental influences, but each problem differed from the other. Allie was an arrogant child, indifferent to the needs or desires of her classmates. When her teacher tried to draw her into room activities, Allie made her attitude very plain. Kindergarten was a place she would attend when she felt like it, but her mama said it wasn't important, she wouldn't learn much there anyway. Her mama said she didn't have to do a thing she didn't want to. (Allie *never* wanted to do constructive things. She was an expert at creating calculated disturbances.) Allie informed her teacher that she would go to first grade in a private school and nothing she learned in kindergarten could be of value *there* anyhow.

A conference with Allie's mother revealed her to be a larger, more fluent edition of the child, with the same arrogance and intolerance of the public school kindergarten. *She admitted that the little girl's attitude was a reflection of her own* but seemed amused at the problems it created in the classroom. All the teacher's efforts to establish rapport with either Allie or her mother were fruitless. She succeeded in getting half-hearted cooperation from the child, but Allie's interest lacked the enthusiasm of most kindergartners.

Morton was the spoiled son of an over-protective mother. He kicked and screamed every day when she brought him to school. For the first week his mother sat in the room with him, for he ran after her every time she tried to leave and his shrieks disturbed the whole school. His mother often kept him at home because, as she admitted, she "got lonesome and wanted his company." His father was dead, and the mother soothed her own loneliness by keeping Morton dependent upon her. All his teacher could do for Morton was to make his hours in school so happy that he would insist on attending, to make him feel that his contribution was so necessary to the room that he must not be absent unless he was ill.

In Morton's case his disruptive behavior seemed almost to be play-acting in response to his mother's cues. When she professed to "need" him, he would respond by sobbing to go home with her. He reacted just as quickly to the pleasure of his teacher and classmates when he came to school, and seemed genuinely interested in all the projects that claimed their attention. His particular problem, created by his mother, was a grave one because she refused to admit that her possessiveness was making him revert to infantile behavior.

Emil was a slow learner, a child of very wealthy parents. They expected great accomplishments from their son. His ivy-league school had already been chosen, they planned that he should join his father in a highly successful business as soon as he was grown. It never occurred to either of his parents that they need question the child's ability to fit into a simple kindergarten situation or respond to the most ordinary learning activities.

His teacher helped Emil to fit into his group, to make small contributions of which he could be proud. She made sure that his learning attempts met with some measure of success. She helped him to progress at his own speed, so that he would have a happy feeling of accomplishment. All this was consideration for the little boy's limited abilities. When the first report of progress was to be made to his parents, his teacher asked for a conference with them. It was a stormy interview, in which she was informed by his father that he was a brilliant man and Emil was expected to be just like him. Nothing short of perfection would be accepted or tolerated by his parents. They could not admit the fact that Emil was now achieving all of which he was capable.

Emil's behavior underwent a drastic change after that interview. From being an easily controlled, lovable little boy with limited learning ability, he became a real behavior problem. His parents had convinced him that his *teacher* was at fault because he couldn't learn all the things the other children learned. He became impudent to her and aggressive with his classmates. An oft-repeated remark was, "I'll show you dumb kids I'm richer than you are. I can do anything I want. If I don't want to do work stuff in this stinky school I don't hafta."

It took more than half a year to help Emil through this phase of parental pressures, when his parents demanded that he perform in the unreal world of their expectations, and his disruptive behavior was the child's only answer to his bewilderment. His teacher had to patiently build up his confidence once more, by helping him to achieve all that she asked of him. This, of course, was very little, but Emil's belief in himself was restored and his behavior improved.

Cultural Contradictions

Contradictions of home and school environment can cause reactions of many kinds in young children. One child may meet the clean, pleasant, happy ways of school with joyous acceptance and carry over neat habits and good manners into his home life. Another child may meet the contrast of school life with his disagreeable, impoverished home with rebellion that is manifested in temper tantrums, stealing, lying, aggression or suspicion of the new, pleasant world of school. A third child may find the contrast of her two worlds so hard to understand that she takes refuge in shame, timidity or withdrawal. Her attitude is one of hopelessness, she feels she can do nothing right, so she stops trying.

Millie and Jasmin were sisters whose birthdays were only ten months apart. Millie was the younger child, an aggressive, rebellious little girl, always on the defensive. She was a severe behavior problem, always suspicious of the motives of every child in her room, and ready to fight anybody who angered her. She boasted and told impossible stories about what she had or did, where she had been and what she had seen. She would steal anything from the children or her teacher that was small enough to be concealed in her meager garments. Millie seemed to feel that she had a right to anything she was clever enough to steal. She tried to make her life like that of the other children by pretending that it was, in the large fantasies she told. Her aggressiveness was an expression of rebellion against the lack of food, warmth and pleasures which she saw other children enjoy.

After a time Millie responded to her teacher's love and understanding. Her attitude of belligerence changed when she found that the children in her room liked her when she was a pleasant playmate. A little success and praise made her become positively angelic, a model of good behavior when her efforts were praised and she could compete on an equal basis with other children. Millie's good behavior, however, was always delicately balanced on acceptance and she would revert to her sullen, suspicious, troublesome attitude when she was unhappy. A child like Millie has great potential for growth and learning, but she can be a real challenge to a teacher.

Her sister Jasmin was gentle and sweet. She wanted desperately to be a clean, ladylike little girl. The dirty clothes she was obliged to wear, her lack of money to pay for the milk she drank, her inability to learn easily, all combined to be more than Jasmin could combat. She was a transfer from another school, repeating kindergarten, and her withdrawn attitude and lethargy seemed to indicate, at first, that Jasmin was a slow learner.

Pretty dresses, coats and shoes were provided for both little girls. Jasmin's teacher encouraged her to perform little tasks in the room and she was given much love and praise for her gentle, thoughtful ways. The children admired her creative art work, they found her to be a good helper in the room, and they often chose her in games. Jasmin's ability to learn increased with her new confidence that she was important to her group. Her lethargy disappeared, and a bright-eyed, eager child attacked each new learning experience with genuine fervor.

Child's Adjustment to the Group

The teacher's attitude toward a child who persistently misbehaves is a guide to the attitude his classmates will have toward him. She should be gentle and kind, but *firm,* so the child who is misbehaving will know that she loves him but expects acceptable behavior from him. Her attitude helps him to realize that he must behave so that other children can enjoy activities in the room without being disturbed by his antics.

Bart was an only child and a very intelligent little boy. From the first day of school he annoyed other children. They reported on his activities, but he was clever in his mischief. It was some time before his teacher saw him slyly pinching his neighbors as they rested on rugs. He tripped his classmates and pushed them into walls.

Talking to Bart was useless for he pleasantly denied any knowledge of wrongdoing. His teacher resorted to removing his chair to a place away from the group. There he could not annoy other children but could participate in the group's activities. He was required to play alone until he felt that he could return to group play without hurting anyone. After a few weeks Bart asked to be allowed the freedom of the room. His behavior was excellent.

One day his mother came to visit school. Bart's difficulties had not been mentioned to her, since his problem had been one that the teacher could solve without a teacher-parent conference. Before his mother left that morning she said, "Could you show me the little boy named Tommy? Bart has told me so much about him."

"What has Bart told you about Tommy?"

"Oh, that he's so naughty in school and has to sit alone, because he hurts other children."

"We don't have a Tommy in this room," the teacher explained. "Bart has been telling you about his own behavior problems."

Obviously Bart had felt the need to "confess" to his mother, after he had learned acceptable behavior. Young children sometimes want reassurance from someone they love, and will go to great lengths to make sure that their misconduct is discovered, even punished, by that person. Adolescents, too, often measure their parents' love and concern for their welfare in terms of the rules their parents have established for conduct and obedience, and the way they enforce those rules. Even very young children want to know what is expected of them, what the rules are. Sometimes in exasperation a teacher will say, "Johnnie, what did you do *that* for?" and Johnnie replies with the utmost honesty, "You didn't tell me not to." Reasonable, clearly understood rules of behavior are a good and necessary part of kindergarten.

Child's Need to Prove Teacher's Love and Tolerance

A teacher is often baffled by a child's persistent misbehavior and by her inability to deal with his problem in the calm, kind way she usually finds to be effective. A particular child may grow increasingly hard to handle and be deliberately provoking her to the point of administering punishment. This conduct may seem unreasonable in a young child and he is obviously quite unaware of the needs that prompt his actions. What the child unconsciously demands of his teacher is, "How much do you love me? How much of my naughtiness can you take? *I want to know.*"

Hans was a boy who needed to know. His home was luxurious, and contained all the physical comforts a child could desire. Hans wanted more than a good bed, warmth, food and an abundance of toys. His father was so busy making money that he had no time for his family. His mother had quietly retreated from loneliness into the life of an alcoholic. Hans couldn't communicate with his mother. She was as elusive as smoke when he made demands upon her. When he was good she didn't notice him. When he was very bad she didn't care. Nothing he did brought a response from his mother. In desperation the child turned to an adult who might answer his burning desire to be noticed and worried about. *He began to torment his teacher.*

He became the most disruptive child she had ever encountered. She employed every trick she knew to control him and nothing helped. One day, when his behavior was particularly outrageous, his teacher abruptly changed her tactics. She unceremoniously walked the astonished Hans out of the room into the hall, beyond the hearing of his classmates. She sat down on a bench facing Hans, put her hands firmly on his skinny little shoulders and looked sternly into his eyes.

"Hans, I am *very* angry at what you just did. If you ever do such a thing again, I will punish you!"

Hans' eyes grew very bright.

"Would you spank me?" he asked her.

"I have never spanked a little boy, but I've never had a boy do what you just did, either."

"You mean I'm sort of special?"

His blue eyes were enormous, his thin little body tense with eagerness.

"You're *very* special." His teacher pulled him close for a brief hug. "Now go inside. I must stay out here a moment until I get over my anger."

Hans said, "O.K. Do you like me, Teacher?"

"I like you very much, even when you're naughty. But you're much easier to love when you behave yourself."

He started through the door but a second later a happy little face peered out at her.

"You know what? I like you, too!"

What a Teacher Can and Should Do upon Recognizing a Child's Severe Behavioral Problem

Most severe behavioral problems are found among emotionally disturbed children. A teacher can help such a child if he is socially unaccepted. He needs to be with people. If she can give him a feeling of belonging, of being an accepted member of a group, she has contributed to his mental health. Giving praise and approval are necessary obligations of the teacher in her treatment of disturbed children. They should be allowed to feel at ease with her, even if they are impelled to hurt her in an attempt to prove her love and acceptance of them.

The wise teacher will never force a child to do something which he feels he cannot do, but instead will help him to build up the necessary skills and courage to do the task. Establishing rapport between herself and the child is an excellent way to help most behavioral problems and the teacher should use various ways to set up this easy relationship. The child's interests can be appealed to, and he must feel that his teacher accepts him. She is his friend. She is trying to help him to rid himself of his worries and tensions.

The knowledge that she may not accomplish too much with him should never keep a teacher from expending every effort to make a troubled child feel wanted, loved and accepted. He should feel a member of the group whenever possible, with the same privileges but also the same restrictions. The teacher can find ways to fulfill his need for status in dramatizations, in role-playing, in performing special tasks. To some children independence and personal pride is first realized in the classroom. The school becomes a refuge, the teacher the instrument of his satisfaction in belonging, of fulfillment.

In summary, teachers should realize that many young children have grave emotional problems which cause disruptive behavior. Helping a child to overcome some of these problems while he is very young is of paramount importance. If a teacher can help a child to have faith in himself, can give him the knowledge that she values him, then he may have the courage to meet his problems.

8

Individual Differences and How to Cope with Them

A kindergarten teacher once said, "When I look at my class on the first day of school I am reminded of my grandmother's flower garden. She loathed orderly rows of bloom and planted her seeds helter-skelter, with a fine disregard for the size a plant might attain when it reached full maturity. Her sturdy, brilliant zinnias flourished among low-growing verbena and candytuft. Her dainty lobelia, that needed a border to show off its delicate beauty, was almost smothered in the brilliant petunias that just 'took over.' As a child I asked her, 'Gram, why don't you plant your seeds so the large flowers can grow at the back, the border flowers at the edge and the middle-sized flowers in between? Your garden would look better.' Gram's answer has occurred to me many times since. 'This world isn't orderly and the people in it aren't, either. The quiet folks who would like to be on the edge of things have to rub shoulders and compete with the out-going, loud ones. Folks have to battle for their place in society, so why shouldn't flowers battle for their place in the sun? I value my flowers more because they have to be strong to grow.'

"Her philosophy is the one I use when I teach my kindergartners. Each child is different, the color of his personality vivid in his own individual way, his character a result of the way he has been nurtured physically and emotionally before he reaches me. As a teacher it is my duty and privilege to help each child find new strength and growth in learning, whatever his mental, physical and emotional capabilities."

Children's interests, abilities and contributions are vastly different. The good teacher knows that the learner brings into the classroom his own potentials, aspirations, and values. She avoids asking for conformity of achievement, but treats each child in her room as an individual, with the right to solve his problems in the way best suited to his needs and capabilities.

Cutts and Moseley have said, "It is important for the teacher to remember that children, like flowers, do not all bloom at the same time, but all need constant nourishment in order to come to bloom at all." [1]

Teacher's Warm Acceptance of Every Child Imperative

The teacher knows, when she looks into the faces of the new kindergartners on the first day of school, that each child will differ as greatly from his neighbor as the delicate points of snowflakes differ. Her responsibility is to learn all she can about these differences. She must find out each child's particular needs and help him to reach his individual potential.

Every day she must offer him her unqualified love and acceptance, must help him to feel that without him her days would not be complete. Without his contribution her class could not proceed in normal fashion. As one small kindergartner earnestly told his mother, "I gotta go to school today and learn stuff. My teacher *needs* me. She said so." A teacher's warm acceptance of a child is the best basis for learning.

Acceptance does not mean permissiveness or lack of discipline. It does not mean that a child will always succeed in school, that he will always be completely happy; but it does mean that

[1] Norma E. Cutts and Nicholas Moseley, *Providing for Individual Differences in the Elementary School* (Englewood Cliffs, N.J.: Prentice-Hall, Inc., 1960).

he will be able to accept discipline, unpleasantness, disappointments, even defeat, without anger, tension or fear if he loves and trusts his teacher. Children like the security of the room whose teacher expects their best behavior, but who still loves them when they make mistakes. Her belief in them helps them to new self-acceptance and greater self-control.

Approval and acceptance on the part of a teacher is not always easy to sustain. There are days when one minor kindergarten catastrophe after another has the teacher in such a state of mental and physical exhaustion that she feels she *can't stand* another squirm out of one more urchin! Then, at that desperate moment of her despair, some naughty child who has demanded her exasperated attention all afternoon, sidles up and says, with his engaging, two-teeth-out grin, "Teacher, ain't you glad I came today?"

His teacher reassures him, for it's true! She is glad he came. He needs her, and she needs him, too. Together they are learning a lot in kindergarten.

The young child's first experiences in school serve as a foundation upon which to build all his future years of learning. He must have the satisfactions he finds in his relationships with his teacher and classmates to strengthen his belief in his own ability. He must have new and exciting experiences to gain knowledge about his world and to ready him for the future.

Recognition of a child's individual differences will help the teacher to give him adequate help in needed areas. His learning and growth progress will then proceed at his own achievement level, its pattern following his own individual requirements.

Children differ in their physical, intellectual, social and psychological characteristics, so the teacher must begin at once to find out as much as she can about each of these areas. Few, if any, records are available for the kindergarten teacher. She may ask help of parents, she may consult the meager information on registration records, but primarily she must study each individual to learn about his needs.

What are some of the questions she asks, as she observes her kindergartners at play, spends some precious time alone with each one, or observes the child in his own home? What does she need to know about the child's physical, emotional, intellectual, social endowments?

The following lists are general, covering the more common areas of individual differences. Each teacher will have specific questions of her own to ask, pertinent to her own problems.

PHYSICAL:

1. Is the child's general health good?
2. Does he fatigue easily?
3. Does he have allergies which may interfere with normal school activities?
4. Is there a sight or hearing difficulty?
5. Is the child physically handicapped in any other way?
6. Does he suffer from hypertension? Is he lethargic or poorly coordinated?
7. Has the child adequate shelter, clothing, food, medical attention? Does he get enough rest?

INTELLECTUAL:

1. Has the child had enriching experiences in his preschool years?
2. Has he a good vocabulary?
3. Does he understand many words which he does not use?
4. Can he express himself verbally? Can he express himself creatively?
5. Has he sound judgment? Good reasoning powers? Does he attack and solve simple problems?
6. Does he have a lively imagination?

SOCIAL:

1. Is the child over-aggressive? Over-confident? Boastful? Do children "report" about his roughness, his selfishness?
2. Does he constantly demand attention?
3. Is he immature, shy?
4. Is he accepted by his peers? Will children work with him? Has he one close friend, many friends, no friends?
5. Is he chosen in games? Do children avoid sitting by him?
6. Is the child culturally deprived? Socially inadequate? Does

he want to make friends but lack the knowledge of how to be friendly?

7. Does he prefer individual tasks or group tasks? Does he avoid any task?

PSYCHOLOGICAL:

1. Is the child's home average-normal or a broken home?
2. What are his relationships with one or both parents?
3. Has he overwhelming fears? Is he afraid of pets?
4. Is the child withdrawn? Does he daydream? Engage in excessive fantasies?
5. Can he play well alone? Has he inner resources or must he be constantly directed?
6. Is his attention span short or sustained?
7. How does the child react to frustrations and disappointments?
8. How does the child think of himself, in terms of *now?* Does he relate things in terms of self, or can he generalize? Can he accept himself and his achievements or is he constantly frustrated and angry at his own inabilities?
9. Does he have an easy, happy acceptance of people and things, or does he rebel against his world?
10. Is he in constant motion? Easily angered? Does he cry often? Does he retreat into uncommunicative silence when his wishes are thwarted?

Individual differences are manifested in all activities in the schoolroom and there are limitless ways in which a kindergarten teacher may respect these differences and still help her children to achieve maximum learning.

When she reads a story, her listeners will interpret that story from their own frame of reference; this is made up of individual background enrichment, physical and mental health, emotional security, understanding of words, meaning and terms used in certain connotations. (In this age of television-viewing, the commercials with their insidious appeal offer new word meanings and associations. The kindergarten teacher often is amused, sometimes alarmed to realize that a story she has read has been completely misinterpreted by her TV-indoctrinated listeners.)

A story which is full of delightful, exciting suspense for the average child, may be full of disturbing horror for the emotionally insecure child. When she has learned to know each child well, the teacher can provide for these differences in her listeners by her choice of story or the way in which she presents it.

She accepts each child as he is, and by her attitude helps him not only to accept himself but to receive the respect of his classmates, whose attitudes tend to reflect those of their teacher. She is aware of the individual differences in her room so she plans many activities, resorts to countless teaching devices and games to help her children accept their differences, to adjust to them; in many cases to completely overcome them. Each child is helped to his own individual, realistic goals. The shy and immature are encouraged to leadership and responsibility. Analyzing *reasons why* some children behave as they do helps the teacher to guide them to new patterns of behavior which make them more acceptable to themselves and to their classmates.

The teacher praises achievement with sensitive awareness of the child's capabilities, commends kind impulses and acts of thoughtfulness. She listens to ideas, rambling thoughts, confidences. There is a comfortable, warm receiving-and-giving relationship between the teacher and child when she thoroughly understands why he is a little different.

A child's special interests can be studied and brought to the attention of his classmates. Even the shy or withdrawn child can express himself when he explains something that interests him, that he knows about. Special efforts can be made to provide materials which will help emotionally disturbed children to express their frustrations or release their tensions. In a room where Leon, a disturbed child, was too frequently aggressive, a work bench was provided, with hammers, saws, nails and wood. Many children in the room enjoyed working there, but it became a special refuge for Leon. There he could pound out his tensions and resentments, could mutilate and destroy boards when his frustrations were more than he could tolerate.

Bobby Joe's home was a disturbed one. His mother was periodically institutionalized for mental illness. Bobby Joe often arrived at school in a state of turmoil which made him nervous, inattentive and withdrawn. When approached by other children he would strike them. He was a creative child and his teacher discovered that working quietly alone, with colored paper, paste and small miscellaneous, textured objects was a therapeutic activity for Bobby Joe. He would emerge from such a work period calm, sweet-tempered, shining-eyed, with several lovely, brightly-colored objects which he would proudly show to the other children.

An area in the room was devoted to creative expression, and many kinds of objects were found there, scraps of cloth, cord, yarn, feathers, pine cones, seeds, seed pods, beans, corn, rice, small stones, paper, paste, and wire. Such an area is a favorite with many children.

Young children can relieve tensions in quiet, sometimes meaningless water play, too, scrubbing the sink, aimlessly washing and rewashing hands, bathing dolls. In kindergarten rooms where space is available, some teachers provide a large tub of water, with small boats to sail about in it. As a child matures he no longer seems to need this kind of activity.

Dramatizations and role-playing are enjoyed by most children. Role-playing is especially valuable as an outlet for the child who constantly needs and demands attention. Children who want to lead and direct others can put their leadership qualities to good use in planning and directing dramatizations, and helping with excursions or field trips.

The physically handicapped child can be drawn into those activities which are especially adapted to his disability and make much of his *capabilities*. Mollie, a crippled child in one kindergarten, always played the role of inanimate objects with verve and enthusiasm. Her classmates praised her performances and insisted that she take part in every dramatization.

A teacher's warm acceptance of all her kindergartners, whatever the nature or extent of their individual differences, is an attitude which is not always easy for her to maintain. She must face her *own* feelings and overcome them, so she will always be able to work and plan for the best interests of her students. If the most aggravating, unpleasant child in her room needs to be appointed "first vice-president-in-charge-of-helping-Teacher," so he will learn good manners and consideration for others, then his teacher will give him the job; not because his conduct has earned the reward of helping her, but because the responsibility will help him to a new concept in social living. She must have the foresight and courage to work patiently with the most disruptive child until she has helped him to acquire new values and new self-respect.

Immature Child and Slow Learner

Some educators call any child a slow learner whose I.Q. is not lower than 75 and not higher than 90; but they qualify this statement by admitting that a child's I.Q. may vary from time to time. A child's mental age must be considered as well as his I.Q. in determining his learning ability. His ethnic, cultural and economic background often affect his ability to learn.

The slow learner is capable of achieving a moderate degree of success in school. He may, however, need more time and individual help from his teacher to acquire basic skills and the confidence to attack problems if he is to progress in ways that are satisfactory to him and to his teacher.

Before she can class a child as a potentially slow learner, before she makes a judgment about a child's ability to learn, there are many factors to be considered. Is the child immature? Has he emotional problems which prevent his learning? Has he a physical handicap which makes learning difficult? Has he been so culturally deprived that he must have time to "catch up" in experience enrichment before he can begin to realize his learning potential? Does lack of proper nourishment make him indifferent and listless? These and many other questions present themselves when a teacher studies the child whose responses *seem* to indicate that he is a slow learner.

On the kindergarten level, with few, if any, records to guide her, the teacher *may mistake the very immature child for a slow learner*. He may have been so over-sheltered at home by parents and siblings that he is reluctant to look after his own needs or to exert himself in any way. He either demands constant attention or sits passively and allows others to do everything for him. Never having been allowed to depend on his own resourcefulness, such a child has to be taught to think and act for himself. He is *not* a slow learner, just a reluctant one.

The child whose body is incessantly active may appear to be a slow learner because he will not give his attention to any quiet activity. When a study of his problems has been made, his teacher may find him to be unusually bright. The *lethargic* child may also appear to have a dull mind, but lethargy, even in the very young, is sometimes a manifestation of hopelessness, of frustration so deeply felt by a child that he takes refuge in indifference. Such an abject retreat into inaction may be a sign of severe mental disorder. In that case, the kindergarten teacher will need to seek professional help. On the other hand, it may merely indicate that a child is clever enough to set up a defensive screen of indifference between himself and the too-alarming demands of adults.

Expectations of over-ambitious parents who insist on a brilliant performance from their child can cause him to react with a show of stupidity. While this kind of behavior is not common among kindergartners, it does sometimes occur when a child is faced with intolerable demands he cannot satisfy.

Children whose homes are culturally deprived may be slow "starters." After they have enjoyed many enriching experiences, they often learn quickly and easily. Judging such a kindergarten child by the usual standards of intelligence-rating would be most unfair.

Slow learners sometimes *but not always* have certain characteristics. They *may* be:

1. Poor in personal and social adjustment.
2. Aggressive, with inacceptable behavior.
3. Quiet and withdrawn.
4. Suffering from failure to achieve.
5. Sensitive to parental expectations.
6. Rejected and in need of security and success.
7. Poorer than average in muscle coordination and development.

There are irrefutable facts about the slow learner. He *does* exist, he is often present in the regular classroom, he *does* need special attention from his teacher so that he may attain certain learning goals. He *does* have difficulty in keeping up with the average learners in his class. He *can* often make valuable contributions to his group, in areas of his special interests.

The slow-learning child draws from past experiences and learns by active participation in new ones, just as all children do. He learns by imitation, by adapting and transferring already acquired knowledge to new situations. He may not be able to reason as well as many of his classmates, and he may not be good at simple problem solving. Sometimes the slow learner observes new activities until he understands what he sees; but a few may plunge into unfamiliar activities in an attempt to win the acceptance of their group. Some slow learners can accept responsibility and will persist in giving the assigned task their best efforts, while many will not accept responsibility at all.

When he receives praise and encouragement from his teacher and classmates, the slow learner acquires a new self concept. This praise convinces him that he, too, is doing something worthwhile. The more he is encouraged, the harder he tries and is able to learn. He sets new goals for himself, and has the confidence to achieve these goals.

His teacher must be a steady, comforting influence. She shows the slow learner why it is important that he learn certain facts and skills. She arranges ways which will allow him to use this knowledge in ways that are pleasant and satisfying to him. If the child reaches a plateau where achievement seems impossible, his teacher must then sustain his belief in himself. She praises his efforts and his courage to attack such difficult problems. Her warm interest and her sympathy with his struggles will do much to help him bear disappointments and failures.

All children "learn by doing" but slow learners need, more than others, to deal with tangible things, to see, hear, touch, taste, smell, to have experiences which they can identify with their own pleasurable activities. Generalizations mean little to the kindergartner who is a slow learner. He needs to handle, to perform, to participate, to be actively engaged in experiences to receive maximum learning. These experiences should involve him physically as well as mentally, when possible. Activities must be simple and easily understood, the plans which he helps to make must be clear and uncomplicated, one sequence following another in simple fashion, all details worked out step by step. He finds security in order and repetition and is sometimes frightened and bewildered by the need to make decisions or to solve simple problems which seem to threaten his safety and well-being. Learning experiences, for him, must be those with which he can identify and which he can quickly use in his daily life. Knowledge gained from such experiences tends to remain with him and becomes part of his mental growth and development.

Over-aggressive Child

The child who fights constantly, who seeks excitement in taunting his companions, who torments children smaller than himself is a troubled child. Something in his world has disturbed him so deeply that he must take refuge in belligerence and fighting, which he enjoys, to compensate for other pleasures which he has been denied.

All teachers have the over-aggressive child in their rooms at some time in the school year. In the kindergarten his companions may not understand his aggression, and meet it with tears, matching aggressions, withdrawal from the child, or, in extreme cases, a flat refusal to attend the school where an over-aggressive child threatens their happiness. The kindergarten teacher sometimes receives a note from a parent, stating that, "Benjamin cries every day when it is time to start to school. Tom Dolan picks on him, kicks him, and threatens to beat him up. Please see that Tom Dolan leaves Benjamin alone." She may receive other notes, from other parents, complaining about Tom. One of them may say bluntly, "My kid don't want to come to school as long as Tom Dolan is there. I won't make him."

His teacher has talked to Tom, she has observed his behavior, and has been trying various ways to reach the child. Her methods of control have been ineffective, for she has not yet discovered *why* Tom Dolan behaves as he does. He is a bright, alert boy, he learns easily. Then she has a conference with his mother and nearly all the puzzling facts about Tom are cleared up, so that she has a total picture of this child and his disturbing aggression. His mother frankly admits that he is a problem at home, and in the neighborhood. She was sure he would be at school and had avoided contacting his teacher. Tom kept his sister in tears and children would not play with him.

"His dad is the same kind of person," she tells the teacher. "He can't keep a job because he won't let folks, not even his boss, tell him what to do. From the time Tommy was a baby his dad taught him to fight, to not take nothing from nobody. Tommy can be real sweet sometimes. He might not be such a mean kid if his dad didn't keep at him to be tough."

Tom could, indeed, be a very "sweet kid" when his teacher approached his problem in a new way. She began to praise his good work, and to encourage his intense curiosity about transportation, space travel, machines. He was encouraged to work at projects which involved simple machines, and to share his knowledge and enthusiasm with other children. Common school interests helped him develop friendships and Tom discovered that he had less desire to fight his companions when they could do interesting projects together. His mother reported that his conduct was somewhat better at home, too, for she was supplying him with materials and he made things that worked. One day his father visited Tom's schoolroom and gruffly commended his teacher for getting the kid "stirred up about inventing stuff." He confided earnestly, "Me, I'm just a working man, no education, and the wife ain't educated, either. We didn't know what to do to keep Tom busy. This here's a smart kid I got and he won't have to take nothing off nobody. *He'll* be a boss!"

Isabelle's over-aggressiveness was the result of a deep feeling of failure. She was a very large child, a slow learner who was not ready for first grade after one year in kindergarten. She was deeply humiliated at being "kept back" in the school she had attended and showed her resentment in extreme over-aggressive behavior toward her teacher and classmates. Isabelle, too, needed love, recognition, new experiences. Because she was older and larger than the other children, she was given the responsibility

NDIVIDUAL DIFFERENCES AND HOW TO COPE WITH THEM   147

of looking after their safety on the playground. She was allowed
o show new students how to use various kinds of classroom
equipment. She quickly realized that a little girl with so much
responsibility, who was so important to her teacher and her
school, must put forth her best efforts. As her self-respect increased, Isabelle's desire to learn was intensified. Her over-aggressiveness had been used as a protective covering for her intense
feeling of inadequacy.

The over-aggressive child often needs friends, he may be an
attention seeker, or he may be an extremely bright child who is
bored and seeks excitement in the disturbance he creates among
his classmates when he torments them. The kindergarten teacher
must have the patience to find the reasons for each child's disturbing behavior, and the kindness and wisdom to help him to
solve his problems.

If a child easily loses self-control she must be ready to keep
him *near* her, so that he will feel secure in her understanding and
tolerance. When he is excessively disturbing she must be ingenious in finding ways to direct his energies into constructive
activities. Fortunately the over-aggressive kindergartner can often
be helped to become a good citizen in the room.

Culturally Deprived Child

The culturally deprived child is found in nearly every public
school. One kindergarten teacher remarked, "*I* never meet any
other kind!" She admitted that there were some advantages to
teaching in a school where all young children lacked enriching
experiences, where vocabularies were limited. Every activity she
introduced was new and exciting, every unfamiliar experience
could be a joyous one.

The teacher who has only a few culturally deprived students
in her room must constantly be aware of their lack of cultural
enrichment and ask herself these questions:

1. Are these culturally deprived children physically well-
   cared for or are they neglected?
2. What games do these children play, and with whom?

3. Have they ever been to church, to a movie, to an amusement park, a zoo, a restaurant?
4. Have they a close relationship with parents, siblings, relatives? Is the home broken?
5. Have these children ever taken a trip? Are they familiar with a train, plane, boat, car, bus?
6. What do my words mean to them when I talk about streams, ponds, rivers, lakes, oceans? Have they any conception of a desert, of sand, mountains, forests, fields, farms?
7. What animals have they seen? Do they know what fish scales feel like? The soft warmth of a puppy's fur? Have they any conception of the size of an elephant?
8. Have they ever been to a party? Had a birthday cake? Colored Easter eggs?

Stories should be carefully chosen to help culturally deprived children acquire background knowledge, while they challenge the interest of the entire group. Film strips are excellent teaching aids, and the kindergarten teacher will want to plan many field trips and excursions. Firsthand experiences and those in which a child may actively participate are valuable ways to enrich any child's background.

The teacher will visit the home of a culturally deprived child if possible, and use the knowledge she gains from such a visit to help the child's adjustment to his school environment. If the home is impoverished (and the child is poorly clothed and undernourished) she may want to ask assistance from any existing school or community agency. If there is unhappiness and cruelty in the home, she can offer the child a wealth of security and personal satisfaction at school. Satisfying experiences at school will not solve all the problems a culturally deprived child must face, but they will help him to find happiness for a part of his day.

A child may arrive at school in the morning, shaking with fright, and report, "My father was beating my sister with a strap, and she was yelling. I saw blood on her arm!" A special effort must be made to soothe and comfort such a child. The home situation seldom changes for her, but school can be a refuge, filled with warmth and security.

When Sidney disobeyed school rules and refused to go home, but insisted on remaining on the playground, his teacher had a quiet talk with him. Why did he refuse to go home?

Sidney's reasons were simple. Home was a place he disliked. His mother worked all day, his father worked early morning hours and got home in the afternoon about the time Sidney arrived from school. His father stopped at a tavern on the way home and he was always drunk. He beat him, the child said, for no reason. If he stayed on the playground, his father would be sleeping when he finally went home. Couldn't he come inside the room and help his teacher after school? His clothes were thin and he got very cold hanging around outside so long, waiting for his father to go to sleep.

Individual differences in children create almost insurmountable problems sometimes; but a teacher makes the effort to help in every possible way.

Children from Ethnic Minority Groups

There are problems peculiar to children from ethnic minority groups which have been discussed in Chapter 2. These refer to that disruptive behavior which results when children are acutely aware of their "differentness" in schools where most of their classmates have another ethnic background.

Few *young* children from ethnic minority groups are guilty of disruptive behavior, however; they may be shy and bewildered, sometimes aggressive, or withdrawn and uncertain, but seldom deliberately troublesome. Such children respond eagerly to their teacher's warm welcome, her immediate interest and her concern in making them an integral part of the kindergarten activities. Their classmates learn to reflect the teacher's attitude, and on the kindergarten level, adjustment in school is easy for children from ethnic minority groups.

In those rare instances when parental prejudices are reflected in one child's reaction to another's poor speech patterns or differently colored skin, the teacher can help that child to overcome his prejudice. One kindergarten teacher used such an instance to develop a learning experience in social living, when a young boy from Thailand became a member of her group. She intrigued the curiosity of her kindergartners by showing them unusual articles made and used in Thailand, and reading stories about the country. Her Thai student eagerly joined the young Americans in planning a study of his country which involved the similarities and differences of games he played, of food he ate, of clothes he wore and songs he sang. All the children were delighted with this experience in learning about each other, and the new student's "differentness" and background were much envied by his classmates.

In parts of the United States the children of migrant workers enter many schools as they accompany their parents across the country in pursuit of a living. Some of these young children speak little or no English, so the kindergarten teacher must help the new student to adjust to an unfamiliar school and an unfamiliar language. If she accepts him as a valued member of her group and lets him share his different and interesting background with his classmates, she can help him to be proud of the color of his skin and his own language. They are part of his individual heritage. Through her kind guidance he can realize that there is no shame in being a member of a minority group.

Brain-damaged Child

The causes and extent of a child's brain damage determine whether the child can become a pupil in the regular classroom. Many children with brain damage attend special schools which are set up to best serve their special learning needs.

Withdrawn Child

There are references to the withdrawn child in earlier parts of this chapter, and to the child who is a slow learner. The withdrawn child may also suffer from severe emotional disorders, or deliberately use his withdrawal into silence as rebellion against conditions he hates.

The kindergarten teacher, faced with a child's continued and complete withdrawal, may try to solve his problems herself. If she realizes the child needs psychiatric help, she may then refer him to the professional help provided by most education systems.

In studying the reasons for a withdrawn child's behavior, his teacher will need to ask for conferences with his parents. Parental attitudes differ toward the withdrawn child. Some parents show great concern toward their child, and offer their complete cooperation; others scoff at the thought that their child is not making a normal response to the people around him, that his withdrawal is a real problem. One parent said, "My kid is just like my father. *He* never talked to anybody, either."

Margery was six years old when she entered kindergarten. Her father brought her to school on the first day and told her teacher, "Margery should've come to school last year, but she won't talk, so we kept her home. She's getting too big to stay home. We don't know what to do with her. You see what you can teach her."

The large child sat quietly day after day without making a sound. She did not voluntarily seek the companionship of her classmates and played alone. When she was asked to perform a task, she complied without any show of interest.

This remote child was an enigma that intrigued her teacher. From her observations she suspected that Margery was intelligent, that her attitude was a passive rebellion against something in her home, perhaps, and carried into her school life. What lay behind the child's determined silence?

Her mother talked quite freely about her. "Sure, we've got seven kids, and Margery is next to the youngest. She was the cutest baby I ever had and the big kids spoiled her rotten. She had a bad sick spell when she was barely three and we had to humor her a lot for about six months. That was a bad time for me to lift her around, for I had this new baby about then. You know, it's a funny thing. Margery talked a lot before she got sick. She's never said a word to nobody since the baby came. Her sickness made her lose interest, sort of."

When questioned further she expressed bewilderment. "No, Margery's illness didn't affect her talking no way, the doctor said. He says she could talk if she wanted to, but she won't make a sound. We've spanked her, and she cries but she won't talk. I don't know what's got into Margery."

At school the child continued to maintain her absolute silence for many months. Her teacher was convinced that the child enjoyed school and might talk with the right incentive.

Further conferences with her mother revealed that Margery's whole life had been changed when the baby came. Her older brothers and sisters played with the infant and had little time for the once-adored "cute" Margery, who had grown into a spoiled, demanding, leggy child of four. When she was no longer an invalid the child realized she was not the center of attention in her home. Since there was no physical reason for Margery's silence and withdrawal, her teacher was convinced that her trouble was an emotional one. Margery had stopped talking and had withdrawn into indifference to punish her family. When parents and siblings removed their adoration from her and transferred it to the new child, she had removed herself from any communication with them.

The teacher was determined to penetrate Margery's silence, to interest her so intensely in some activity that she would break her determined silence and talk. She gave her responsibilities in the room, she allowed the child to work with her after school, to help with many special tasks. Their companionship was an easy one that seemed to please the little girl. On several occasions the teacher was sure that only Margery's very strong will kept her from bursting into speech.

One sunny day in late April the kindergarten class went to visit the zoo. The day before a note had gone home with Margery to get her parents' consent to make the trip, and to suggest that she might like to take a bag of popcorn and peanuts with her to feed the monkeys and the bears.

Margery was in a state of intense excitement that morning as she fed the animals. Her face was flushed and she seemed ready to explode with her pent-up feelings. Back at school, as the bus unloaded its young passengers after the trip, Margery walked about with restless impatience.

When they were alone together Margery put her hand into her teacher's hand. She said, "Thank you, Teacher. All my life I wanted to go to the zoo. I never been so happy before."

As Cutts and Moseley said, "It is important for the teacher to remember that children, like flowers, do not all bloom at the same time, but all need constant nourishment in order to come to bloom at all." [2]

---

[2] Norma E. Cutts, and Nicholas Moseley, *Providing for Individual Differences in the Elementary School* (Englewood Cliffs, N.J.: Prentice-Hall, Inc., 1960).

9

Specific Problems

Involving

Individual Differences

In Chapter 8 the individual differences of kindergartners were discussed in general. Every teacher has encountered, at some time, a child whose "differentness" presented a baffling problem; one that challenged both her understanding and her ingenuity to provide adequate instruction for him while she pursued her regular teaching program for the other children in her room.

The accounts of four children are presented in this chapter, and the ways in which each teacher dealt with the child's individual problem.

"Oh, Look What Albert Can Do!"

Albert was a quiet, good-natured, helpless little boy who allowed other children to wait on him, who never expressed an idea of his own and contentedly did whatever he was told by playmates or adults. He was a slow learner, with poor muscle coordination. He could not comprehend how to turn a coat sleeve that was wrong-side-out, so that he could put on his own coat. Zipping his coat was a task he would not attempt.

For a few weeks the kindergartners treated Albert like a pet, doing things for him, helping him, even dressing him for outdoor play. Their teacher discouraged this constant attention, for Albert was growing more helpless every day. She had started a simple program to help build up his self-esteem, for she had discovered that he had no confidence in himself. He honestly believed that he couldn't do anything, and his passive acceptance said, Why try?

A conference with his mother revealed that Albert's brothers were all adults, and she admitted that she had played with and enjoyed her last baby, born near her middle age, as a little girl would enjoy a doll. "He's always been a cuddly little boy, and he loves to have me do things for him. He'll have a hard enough time when he gets grown up," she explained. "I won't let him lift a finger." She was quite shocked and indignant when his teacher suggested that he needed to rely on himself, to have confidence in his own ability to make decisions and to accept simple responsibilities.

At school Albert was being challenged by simple small tasks that were within his learning limitations. At first he was reluctant to exert himself and smilingly refused to participate in activities. Then the other children began to jeer at him. "What's the matter with Albert?" "Albert can't do anything but baby stuff." "My big brother thinks Albert is *stupid*."

His teacher doubled her efforts to help Albert gain some self-confidence. She praised the small things that he was willing to do and encouraged his classmates to praise him. "Look at this picture," she would say. "Aren't Albert's colors beautiful? Isn't this a happy picture?" A very astute little boy challenged her praise one day. "You don't *really* think Albert's colors are pretty," he said. "You only say that to make him feel good."

"Albert has made a picture which pleases him, so it pleases me, too," she explained. "His colors *are* beautiful to him, and he is happy when I praise them. Patrick, you like to be praised for good work you do, and you could be such a help if you would show Albert how to do some of the things that are so easy for you but so hard for him. Could you teach him to zip his coat?"

Teaching Albert to zip was a difficult job, one Patrick worked at diligently. Other children, not to be outdone by Patrick, undertook to teach Albert other simple skills which he lacked. *Helping Albert to Learn Things* was a kindergarten project initiated by them and quite effective.

"Oh, look what Albert can do!" was a delighted comment often heard in the room as he cautiously began to do things for himself. He built a house with blocks, tidied a toy corner, counted to ten. The children encouraged him. One little girl observed, "Albert, you are learning how to work really hard," when he struggled to trace the letters of his name that she had carefully written for him. Albert's smile was a triumphant one when he achieved some simple goal and he no longer waited patiently to be told what to do, but entered into games and occasionally made an observation or two about how *he* liked to play.

Patrick was very encouraged about his charge and made daily reports about the zipping activity. "Before you know it, Albert will zip, just like that!"

Prompted by the lively interest and encouragement of his classmates, Albert even practiced zipping at playtime, a gesture of perseverance that brought extravagant praise from them. "Look at Albert, *he* even works while we play. *He's* the best worker in the room!"

One morning, during show and tell time, a proud Patrick hustled Albert into his coat, while his teacher and classmates waited expectantly. Then, as if he uncovered a masterpiece, Patrick commanded, "Now, Albert—zip!"

Albert's big grin was radiant. He obviously felt ten feet tall as he zipped and unzipped his coat before his admiring audience.

He was so overwhelmed by his new achievement that he began to boast and swagger a bit. One day his teacher had a report from a patrol leader that Albert had made a very rude and discourteous gesture at a passing lady. When his teacher discussed the incident he admitted, with pride, that he had done it. "Sure, the big boys told me to."

They talked together about the need for a little boy to decide what was right and wrong. He must refuse what big boys asked of him when he knew it was something he should not do. "Do you understand what I am trying to tell you, Albert?" she asked him. He thought about it for awhile. Yes, he agreed, he was ashamed of being rude to a lady. "A boy like you who can copy his own name and zip his own coat is big enough to have nice manners. You can decide how you should act," she reminded him. "You are learning many good things, Albert." "Yeah," he said happily, "all the kids in this room say I am learning good."

Convinced that he was now big enough to make some decisions for himself, Albert began to show an interest in simple reading-readiness activities. His progress was slow, but the harder he tried to learn, and the more he was encouraged by his classmates, the more he was able to learn. He was so eager to receive praise for his industry that he gave up all his free time to play number games with his willing friends. Their "Oh, look what Albert can do!" was such sweet music to his ears that his teacher had to intervene. She reminded him that there was a time for boys to run and play at school, and a time to learn. He needed to do both.

Albert began to carry his new-found self-confidence into other activities. He offered to take care of the fish. He took great pride in helping the children keep their room neat, spending much time picking up scraps of paper carelessly scattered on the floor by his classmates. His teacher was always ready to offer him encouragement, to provide him with new achievement goals which were geared to his limited abilities.

Almost a whole kindergarten year passed before Albert found the courage to stand before his friends and sing alone. He remembered every word of the song and his classmates were generous in their praise. "I'll bet you're especially proud of Albert," Patrick said to his teacher; and she answered, "We are *all* proud of him. Albert has worked very hard to show us how much he can learn."

The Story of Nellie

Nellie's teacher told this story of her experience with the handicapped child.

"Nellie entered the kindergarten room on the first day of school, alone, and without records of any kind. She had not been previously registered, she had not been physically examined by our school nurses in the kindergarten "round-up" which was conducted for pre-kindergarten children every spring. When I asked the child if she had just moved into our town, Nellie's reply was casually profane. She had been in a "* * * hospital" until two days ago. I was startled, for the child looked quite healthy. I decided to question her later, when the other kindergartners were playing, for I had a very large group of children and needed to get an activity started.

"The child's behavior was disturbing from the moment she arrived. She talked loudly, constantly and with such profanity that I knew I must deal with that problem immediately. She teased the smaller children and pushed them around until some were in tears. I observed that she seemed belligerent, her hands were always doubled into fists and I wondered why. I could see that she was very aggressive, but her doubled fists were unnecessary, for no kindergartner dared to stand up to her; instead the children avoided her.

"When we started to make a circle for a group game, I heard a boy say, 'Don't hold that girl's hand. She feels awful!' and a little girl on the other side of Nellie shrank away from her, with an odd look of horror on her face.

"I said, 'Let's all hold hands.' The girl beside Nellie began to cry. 'I won't,' she sobbed. 'She hasn't got real hands. They're hard and funny!'

"Nellie stood there, her face crimson with anger, her body tense. Then she began to strike the children on either side of her, using her clenched fists like clubs. For the first time I closely observed those fists and I began to suspect the pitiable truth.

"When the other children were happily playing, I took Nellie with me into a small adjoining room and asked her to tell me about her hands. She eyed me angrily, suspicious of me at first; then abruptly she thrust them out, horribly scarred and twisted hands that were truly 'not real hands,' as the little girl had said. It took much gentle persuasion to get Nellie to tell me the story of her hands, and it was not complete. I had to fill in the background story, the way in which she had been injured, from information I received later from her mother.

"Now, however, she told me in her violent, profane way that she had been in and out of a children's hospital ever since she could remember, that they hurt her there, her hands and her legs. She showed me where skin had been taken from her legs and thighs to be grafted on her hands. They hurt her so bad she hated *them*, she hated other kids, she hated her folks and she hated me, too, she added defiantly.

"I made a visit to Nellie's home and her mother talked freely about her. The sheet-iron, wood-burning stove in the living room was the one she'd run into, her mother explained. She had been playing, stumbled and put out both hands to catch herself, but fell into the red-hot stove and was dreadfully burned. Most of the burns had healed but her fingers were drawn, her hands scarred. The grafting work done on them was tediously slow and very painful.

" 'Someday they think to get her fingers straightened out,' the mother explained. 'But she hates to go to the hospital so bad, I don't know if she'll go when she gets bigger. She's stubborn and mean. She's getting so we can't make her mind. I don't know how you can put up with her at school. I wish I could help, but I've got my own troubles, too.'

"Nellie's problems involved all us at school. She seemed determined to make our lives miserable because she was miserable. She strongly resisted my attempts to make her a part of our group. On the first day that she was absent from school I told the kindergartners the story of Nellie's injury and explained that the pain and trouble she had endured made her so unhappy that she was sometimes unpleasant to us. We agreed that we would all try to help her to be a happier girl.

"When she returned to school I suggested that the children would be interested in having her tell them about what was being done to her hands. Would she share her hospital experiences? I made this suggestion with some trepidation, for the profanity still popped out when Nellie was excited.

"After some thought Nellie agreed to talk about her stay in the hospital, and I was gratified that she chose her words carefully and was not bitter about her treatment. She let the children touch the hard skin on her palms. Afterwards she seemed pleased that she had been the center of their attention. Now that the children understood all about her hard, clenched hands, they no longer rejected her, and some of them were especially kind and thoughtful, holding small things for her which she could not pick up or hold for herself.

"I gave her many responsibilities in the room and discovered that Nellie enjoyed being helpful. She was bright and learned easily; she made suggestions about activities, some of which were excellent.

"Nellie's disposition did not change overnight, however. There were times when she seemed deliberately to try every ounce of patience her classmates and I could muster; it was then I had to agree with her mother. 'Nellie is mean.' Sometimes she showed a sweetness that encouraged me to believe she would overcome her hatred of the people in her world.

"In February she went back to the hospital for more treatment. I gave her a folder of games and projects to work on when she felt well enough, and many of the children brought small gifts so she could have toys to amuse her. She was so astonished at their thoughtfulness that for once in her life Nellie was speechless!

"She returned to school three weeks before school was out. I was afraid her experiences in the hospital might have made her revert to her belligerence and suspicion of us, but Nellie seemed happy to be back. She proudly showed me the folder I had given her and pointed out that she had played every reading-readiness game and every counting-experience game. 'They're right, too,' she informed me. 'The nurses said so.'

"After the other kindergartners had gone home that day Nellie remained to talk to me. 'Look,' she said, showing me one hand. 'See that finger? It's getting *straight!* Someday I'll have five fingers like any other kid, and I'll be the best writer in school!'

"I knew, then, that Nellie's mother need not worry about her refusing to go back. This child was determined to have five good fingers with which to write! I must continue to challenge her in every possible way, for she was very alert and eager to learn.

"On the last day of school, when I said goodby to Nellie and told her what a good first-grader I knew she would be, she looked at me solemnly. 'I won't ever be a beauty queen, my pop says, with these scars on my legs,' she said, 'but I can be the smartest kid in school if I try, I'll bet.' Then, in her excitement Nellie got quite carried away. 'I'll be so smart,' she assured me, 'that I'll be a *** *** school teacher, just like you!' "

The Story of Darwin, an Anecdotal Record

When a kindergarten teacher enrolls a withdrawn child as a member of her class, she may want to keep a detailed account of his behavior. This history of his problems, his reactions to school situations, the methods she has used to help him, the ways in which she has *failed* to reach him, will serve to assist her in making further plans for the child's particular problems. If there are counselors in the school system, this detailed account of a child's behavior will help them to make judgments on him; it will also serve as a guide in discussing the child's school difficulties with his parents.

The following account is an anecdotal record of one withdrawn child. There was no counselor in the school system, so his kindergarten teacher sought help from her principal and the child's parents. Many of her day-by-day observations have been deleted from this case history for reasons of brevity, but all the necessary information for a summation of the case has been presented.

September: When Darwin's mother enrolled him in kindergarten she explained that he is a very strange child. Last year, in Texas, his nursery-school teacher recommended psychiatric help for him, but his parents would not permit him to have help; they felt it would brand him as "queer."

October: For more than four weeks Darwin has not voluntarily entered the room. I have to lead him in, and put him in his seat.

Early November: Darwin now enters the room without urging, but stands and stares, waiting to be invited to his seat. I am kind and loving, I try to make room activities attractive to him, so he will want to participate. He will not respond to me, or to the children.

Mid-November: Darwin will get paper and sit alone, making

detailed drawings of easily identified objects. I praise them, and display them. The other children admire them. He follows directions well, he is usually obedient, but he does not talk. He only stares at us. He insists on sitting alone, he plays alone. He never speaks or smiles.

December: Today, while we were playing a counting game, Darwin came to me and mouthed some unintelligible words in my ear, which I assumed were the names of numerals. I showed him that I was pleased. He now answers my direct questions by nodding or shaking his head. He has not spoken aloud. His mother, in one of her hasty visits to school, says he has a bad speech impediment. She does not expect him to talk to me.

February: For the first time since school began in the fall I have had a real conference with Darwin and his mother in the kindergarten room. I have often asked for conferences with her, or with both parents, but she has ignored my requests entirely, or excused herself because she has a small infant; and her husband because he won't admit that Darwin's behavior is unusual, so sees no need to talk with a kindergarten teacher about his son.

Before his mother arrived I took Darwin with me to the school storeroom. We communicated all the way through the long hall— I talked, *he* nodded. When we got to the storeroom I let him select bright colored paper to use for a project in our room. Once, in answer to a question, he whispered "Yes."

The conference was not a satisfactory one. His mother forced him to say hello to her, but it was only a mouthed response to her urging and not a genuine greeting. Later he made barely audible answers of "no," "yes" and "I don't know" to her persistent questions.

She insists that Darwin sings at home the songs that I teach all the children, and sings them in tune. She says he likes one kindergarten boy. (I have never seen him near this child.)

Late February: Today I went to Darwin's home for a conference. His mother was very nervous and apologetic for her sparsely furnished living room. She confessed that she had not asked me to visit before because she was ashamed of her home. Darwin seemed pleased to have me there. He showed me a watch, his cars and toys. His mother told me he liked pets. She also talked about some "traumatic" experiences which Darwin and his brother had had in Texas. She seemed much more concerned about her own loneliness, her own feelings than those of her son.

The next day: Today Darwin sought out a boy playmate for the first time since school began. (Not the boy his mother thought he liked.) The two little boys played together. Darwin often whispered in his friend's ear.

February 27: Darwin is playing with his friend today. I have moved the boys to a table which they may share. They smile at each other, tease each other.

March 12: Today Darwin and Pat included another quiet boy in their games. Darwin teases Pat. He now smiles often and makes funny noises that make Pat and the other children laugh.

March 18: Pat was absent today and Darwin seemed lonely and unhappy. I suggested that he choose some child to sit in Pat's chair near him. He seemed pleased when many children asked him to choose *them*. At playtime Darwin was in the midst of rough boy-play, tumbling, pulling, wrestling, laughing, but *never* talking.

March 20: We have a show and tell time. Darwin wore two large rings, one on each hand. When I commented on them he was pleased. He readily stood up to show them but refused to speak aloud. Later I saw him teasing Pat and Pat looked ready to cry. I believe he hurts Pat deliberately when he feels frustrated about something that has happened.

March 27: Darwin likes books. He does individual reading-readiness work neatly and accurately. He seems very alert mentally and enjoys the number games and experiences we have in the room.

April 2: Today I had another conference with Darwin's mother in their home. Against his father's wishes she has been taking him to a speech therapist, and she fears her husband's anger when he knows what she has done. She talked incessantly about her own unhappiness, her marriage, her husband and their roles as parents. She made remarks like, "What are we doing to our children? I don't know who needs the psychiatrist most, us or our children."

April 17: Today I chose a story to read about a little duck

who refused to speak duck language until he had something special to say. When I finished the story a little girl said, "Darwin is like the duck. He won't talk, either." Another child spoke up, "Darwin can talk. He talks to *me* when me and my mother visit his mother." Someone else said, "Darwin will talk when he has something special to say, I'll bet." Several children chimed in, "Will you, Darwin?" He looked very pleased. He did *not* answer.

April 22: Darwin came to me today and indicated that I was to pull his loose tooth. When I pull a tooth at school I give the child an envelope, and in it goes his tooth and a dime. When I lifted the tooth out, and gave him the envelope I said, "What else did I put into the envelope besides the tooth?" Pat said, "You know Darwin can't say dime."

"Of course he can. Both he and the duck can talk. One of these days Darwin will want to talk a lot, just as the duck did." As the children walked away I saw Darwin give Pat a hard kick on the leg. This child must want desperately to express himself verbally.

April 30: I have had to move Pat to another part of the room, for Darwin has grown very aggressive in his play, as he feels more at ease with the group. Today Pat complained that Darwin was mean to him. "He works me over and wears me out. Can I sit somewhere else?" I explained to Darwin that his rough play hurt his friend. Later I saw him go to Pat, put his arms around him and whisper in his ear.

May 5: Darwin returned to school today after a four-day illness. We all showed him that we were very happy to have him back. Later, when his mother came to pick him up and take him home, he told her, "I feel like I don't want to go home. I like school. I want to stay longer and play with my friends." She ran back to the room to tell me.

May 15: I overheard some children discussing Darwin's refusal to talk. Several boys told about talking with him when they played at his house. Obviously his reluctance to talk in the room is due to his self-consciousness about his bad speech.

May 18: Darwin has been given a reading-readiness test. In a group of forty-seven children he ranks thirty-seventh. His score was 88, the battery median 91. He enjoyed taking the test.

He is still working with the speech therapist. She assures me that there is nothing physically wrong with Darwin to prevent his speaking as well as other children. His poor speech is a bad habit, and he now uses it to escape from having to talk. She also has found, as I have, that he uses violent action against toys as an expression of resentment and frustration. She said, "Darwin's speech difficulty seems to be an outward manifestation of inner emotional involvement."

I feel that Darwin is *now* using his silence as an attention-getter. He enjoys his classmates' concern about him, he enjoys being different.

May 30: I have had very disquieting news. Darwin will move to Florida in July. He will have to make new friends and attend a new school. In spite of his progress, he is still a poorly adjusted child. He has done very good work in reading-readiness activities. His art work shows intelligence and maturity in the way he sees things in his surroundings; however, no child is making normal responses at the age of six, when he refuses to express himself verbally before a group.

Darwin has learned to accept me. His mother say he refers to me at home as "my teacher who *really* likes me." Our year together has not been easy. I have given him love, praise and understanding but I have had to rebuke him often for excessive roughness (in the last few months) and for unkindness to his friend Pat. Darwin seems to need both kinds of treatment and regards them as being necessary to belonging to his group.

I have prepared him for first grade. He has learned to accept disapproval as well as praise. He is now more out-going, more friendly than I ever dreamed that he could be.

To summarize: I must admit the great improvements I find in Darwin's adjustment to people may be only superficial and temporary, for I feel that there is an underlying emotional disturbance behind his still-deviant behavior. If he could remain in this school, among his new friends, I believe he would make steady progress toward a normal acceptance of his world. Since his family is moving to a new community, Darwin will have to make new adjustments in many phases of his life. (He has already moved seven times in his six years, each time to a different state.)

He may react to this change by reverting to the remote, withdrawn, blankly staring little boy who entered school last fall. Anything I may have done for Darwin is not apt to carry over into his new life unless the happy experiences he has recently had in school have made a more lasting impression on him than I realize.

The Story of Barry

Jane Smith was an experienced kindergarten teacher and often remarked that she had taught children with as many kinds of individual differences as were known to man. Just name it, she'd had it! That was before Barry came to her room.

There was nothing in his appearance or behavior to tell her that he would present a greater challenge than any student she had taught. Barry was a handsome child, quiet, a little immature, with gentle manners and a pleasant disposition. The children liked him.

She had a very large group of kindergartners that year, and they were all so full of curiosity and eagerness to learn that Jane Smith's days were unusually busy, as she devised ways to challenge and stimulate the kindergartners' alert minds. She congratulated herself that there wasn't a single serious problem in the entire group; all normal as sunshine, bless them.

After a few weeks she observed a change in Barry's even temper. He was often cross and irritable, and seemed bewildered when she asked him questions about activities they had enjoyed together when he first came to school. He was not as quick to learn as the other students, but he enjoyed stories, songs and dramatizations, he loved to play simple games, he followed directions as easily as any child, he seemed to understand kindergarten activities. What was troubling Barry?

Close observation of the little boy at play convinced Jane Smith that his problem was an unusual one. When her children had an exciting and enjoyable experience one day, they would always want to repeat it the next day, or have a similar one. To Barry every experience was *new*. He did not carry over knowledge from one happening to another, made no association between an experience he might have had on Tuesday and an almost identical one on Wednesday. Situations were set up to test his memory of factual material, and he reacted to these activities with uncertainty and tears.

Then Jane Smith realized that Barry had no power to recall any experience of a purely mental nature, but when he participated physically in a game his body responded to the previously experienced activity and by watching closely he could soon follow the rules of the game.

She sent Barry's mother an urgent request for a conference. Jane Smith, who thought she had met every individual difference in the book, had encountered a new and very baffling one.

Both parents came to the conference, both were very helpful in explaining Barry's background. He had been quite ill with encephalitis when he was three years old. The attending doctor told his parents then that he had suffered brain damage, but the exact extent of this damage was not known. The doctor surmised that the specific nature of the damage would manifest itself when Barry started to school. He urged that the child's teacher *not* be told about his previous illness, but be allowed to discover for herself in what way Barry's brain injury affected his learning patterns.

His parents were grateful for her interest and agreed to help Barry in any way they could. Immediately after the conference he was given extensive examinations by specialists and when the reports came back his mother relayed their information to his teacher. Jane Smith had been right in believing that Barry lacked the ability to recall simple factual experiences. His doctors offered some hope that his memory might improve as he matured. They recommended that he live a normal life, participate in all kindergarten activities, and be allowed to enjoy and learn as much as he could.

Both his parents and his teacher realized that he would need to spend two years in kindergarten, but Jane Smith was determined to make those years happy and exciting ones for this little boy to whom every experience was so new. She planned his learning experiences so they would involve physical as well as mental activity; she adroitly guided him so that he no longer felt frustrated and angry when he "forgot." She helped her kindergartners to accept his absence of memory as something that set him apart from the rest of them in a special way, just as Bill's bright red hair and Betty's brown skin made them special, too.

On the first day of his second year in kindergarten, Barry greeted his teacher with pleasure, and she watched him walk about the room, touching favorite toys. Could he remember them from last year? As she taught the flag salute to her new kindergartners Barry listened, wide-eyed. "One of these days I'll say that all by myself, and you won't have to help me," he told her.

He began to bring books to her. "Have I ever seen this book before?" Jane Smith assured him that the book's story was a favorite of his. He turned the pages and his eyes began to sparkle. "I think I know. It's about the elephant who wouldn't mind his mother!"

She gave Barry many responsibilities that year and made him feel that she was very proud of the learning efforts he made. She devised ways to unobtrusively test his ability to follow directions, his perception, his reasoning powers, his memory of happy experiences. Sometimes he would ask, in a puzzled, hopeful way, "Have I ever done this kind of work before? Have I ever played these games with numerals?"

To such questions Jane Smith would respond warmly, "Oh, yes, Barry, you have. We did this last year, remember, when you . . ."

There were still many times when he would have no recollection of the experiences she mentioned; but he was never allowed to feel unhappy or frustrated because he could not remember. She found ways instead to strengthen his belief in his increasing *ability* to remember past knowledge and past experience.

Barry went to first grade the following year. Learning was difficult for him, but his parents were wise and helpful in handling his problem; and his progress, though slow, was steady.

One more challenging individual difference problem had been added to Jane Smith's experience as a kindergarten teacher. She and Barry had both learned much from their two years together. She treasured, too, a letter of gratitude from Barry's parents, which said in part, "without an early understanding of his problem, and your constant, specialized help to guide his first efforts in school, Barry's whole life might have been one of disappointment and frustration."

Other Examples

Kindergarten teachers must be free to arrange their programs and activities to the individual needs of their pupils when children with severe physical handicaps are admitted to the kindergarten. Teachers must be sensitive to their needs and proficient in ways to meet them, so the children can make contributions to the group and find acceptance among their classmates. Children with severe hearing or sight losses, however, need specialized help and their teachers should join the parents in seeking such assistance from available sources if they are to have the best learning opportunities. However willing she may be, the average teacher is not trained to teach the child with severe sight or hearing loss.

Left-handed children often present a problem to the kindergarten teacher. She must confer with the child's parents and find answers for many questions. Should the child be allowed to continue his left-handedness, or should the teacher attempt to change him? Should she encourage a child to be ambidextrous? If a left-handed kindergartner persists in "smudging" his work because of the position in which he holds his crayon or paint brush, what can she do to help him acquire work habits that will make writing skills easier? How can she provide good classroom environment for the left-handed child?

The very bright or the gifted child often has serious adjustment problems on the kindergarten level. Chapter 11 in this book is devoted to the bright or gifted child, so discussion here is not necessary.

Every kindergarten teacher has met, or will meet, children like Albert, Nellie, Darwin or Barry, whose problems were presented in detail. The child may be dark or fair, thin or plump, but his needs are essentially the same. Teachers should be able to recognize those children who are emotionally insecure, withdrawn, or inept and immature; they should ask themselves if the boy who is a bully and a braggart acts as he does because he desperately wants friends and does not know how to make friends. They should understand the little girl who is jealous of her younger sister, and the shared experiences she is having with mother at home. She cannot bear to leave them there together, so feigns illness or has tantrums when she is forcibly brought to school.

Teachers learn to accept the individual differences of children in their rooms. The special case histories in this chapter were presented *not* to say, "This is the way such a child *should* be treated," but perhaps to suggest, "Albert, Nellie, Darwin or Barry responded to a certain kind of treatment. A boy called John may have a problem different from any of these, but a similar approach to his problem might work for John, too."

10

The Importance of
Parent-Teacher Interviews
in the
Kindergarten

The kindergarten teacher plays an important role in the life of the young child. During preschool years his home and parents, his brothers and sisters have been the center of his whole world. Now, with the beginning of his school life, another adult claims his interest, his allegiance, sometimes his unreserved adoration. He believes every word she says, he quotes her constantly, to the dismay of his parents sometimes; and he may persist in doing "what my teacher says," in spite of established beliefs and practices which are observed in his home.

Throughout a child's life his parents and teachers are striving to reach the same goal for him, to make his life happy, secure and abundantly rich with learning experiences. They all help to mold the child into a future good citizen, so they should work together, when possible, to find patterns of intellectual growth best suited to that individual child.

In establishing a successful working partnership with parents the kindergarten teacher needs to be very understanding of the parents' objectives for their child. She must be tolerant of all parental views, even those that widely differ from her own; she must try to understand and sympathize with their concept of their child's potentials and abilities. If she finds parents to be intolerant, immature, prejudiced, even antagonistic toward schools and their objectives, she will feel concern for their opinions; but she can exercise patience and ingenuity in helping them to an understanding of the ways in which their child's school is prepared to meet his various needs.

One excellent way in which a teacher can establish rapport with parents is to let them know that she *needs* their help. Theirs can be a working partnership and she genuinely desires their interest and cooperation. She can show them that ideas and creative suggestions for their child's intellectual growth and physical welfare can be shared, and that she is receptive to their ideas.

There are many ways in which the kindergarten teacher may meet and confer with parents. Some schools provide for kindergarten "open-house" teas or meetings, where parents can meet their child's teacher, and the teacher can acquaint them with the kindergarten's objectives. Conferences and interviews can be arranged for at a later date, when the teacher has become acquainted with the child. Helpful questionnaires are sometimes sent out by the teacher, asking parents if the child likes school, which activities he enjoys, what his reactions are to other children. Arranged home visits, at a time when the teacher can meet both father and mother, are excellent ways in which to get acquainted with parents, or to work out solutions to a child's individual problems.

There are a few rules of professional courtesy and good taste which a teacher should use in conducting all conferences or interviews with parents.

The teacher should:

1. Make the atmosphere of the conference natural and pleasant, so parents will feel the desire to talk freely.
2. Emphasize the *good* qualities of the child, focus the entire talk around the child's needs.
3. Try to have the interview in a quiet atmosphere, where

parents and teacher can be relaxed and at ease together.

4. Courteously refuse to discuss a child's problems during school hours when kindergartners are present, but arrange instead for a private conference or home visit.

5. Encourage parents to have an interview at school after hours, if parents seem reluctant or refuse to receive the teacher in their home.

6. Never tell parents *what to do* in relationship to their child, but be prepared to refer parents to specific, specialized helps if they urgently request it.

7. Instill confidence in the parent by warm, genuine concern for the child. When parents feel a teacher is really interested, they will want to approach her with problems.

8. Try to interview parents at a time most convenient for *them,* particularly if their child has a problem about which they might feel antagonistic.

9. Make parents feel that their contribution is valuable, their cooperation vitally important. Try to establish a feeling of mutual liking, confidence and respect. Show them that you want to *help* their child, not to complain about him.

10. Remember that parents have a difficult task in always knowing what is best for the child, in relationship to other children; they need praise and encouragement, just as teachers do.

11. Keep in mind, during an interview, that parents can't always be objective about their child.

12. Be wary of making diagnoses about a child's problems, or of prescribing remedies when parents reveal a bad relationship between themselves and their child.

13. Avoid disgust, dismay or annoyance when discussing a child's unpleasant or unacceptable behavior.

In some schools it is the practice of teachers to visit the home of every child, if possible. Certainly a kindergarten teacher will want and need to visit the home of any child who shows evidences of emotional instability, social inadequacy or maladjustment, or physical disorders. There she may find answers to many questions, such as:

1. What is the emotional atmosphere of the home?
2. Has the child had a normal relationship with siblings?
3. What is the economic and cultural status of the home?
4. What attitudes do the parents have toward school, teachers, education?
5. Do the parents have time to be interested in each individual child in the home? Do they sometimes take time to be alone with a child and give him special attention?
6. Does the child seem to demand an unusual amount of attention at home? Is he smothered in an over-abundance of attention and solicitude which he neither needs nor wants?
7. Are his parents over-protective?
8. Are parents so preoccupied with adult interests that their child cannot identify with them?
9. If a child has deviant behavior, are the parents unable to accept it?
10. What are the attitudes of siblings and relatives toward the deviant child?
11. Do the parents accept a physically handicapped child, an emotionally perturbed child? Do they try to "explain away" the difficulty by fixing blame on heredity, on family misfortunes, on an absent parent (in the event the home is a broken one)?
12. Have the parents evinced reluctance to have a child's disability checked because: examinations are too costly; what they don't know for sure doesn't worry them; they simply lack interest in finding help for the child? Do they accept the child's handicap but refuse to seek help for the child because of a religious belief?
13. Do the parents pressure their child because he does not perform in a manner which satisfies their expectations? Do they compare the child's achievement to other members of the family, or to those of neighborhood children?
14. Are the parents too permissive with their children, do they fail to show enough concern for their children's behavior?
15. Does the child feel rejected by either parent, by both parents?

When a teacher makes a home visit, these are some of the questions about the child which she hopes to have answered. Observation of the home will often give her the information she needs. Her adroit and pleasant questioning of the parents will sometimes elicit answers which help her to solve the child's problems. With this information she is able to work more effectively with this particular child.

The teacher should always be careful about evaluating the home from a single visit. She must never discuss what she has observed, or reveal confidences with which she has been entrusted, (unless this information is given to a counselor for guidance purposes; even then, it is a good idea to ask the parents' permission).

If the conditions of a child's home are antisocial, brutal, sordid, if a foreign language and foreign ways impede the child's adjustment to school; if the whole atmosphere is one of suspicion and antagonism toward teachers, schools, and the community, then the teacher may never be able to effect changes in the child's life at home. She can, however, make use of her knowledge of his home environment to provide him with happy and satisfactory experiences at school. She can build up his confidence in his ability to effect changes in his own life, she can help him to success in achievement. Her appreciation and love can in some measure compensate for the lack of parental interest and security in his home.

When parent conferences and home visits have revealed a child's special needs, the teacher can more effectively help him to find fulfillment and satisfaction in the activities she provides for him at school by giving him praise and approval, and by allowing him to discharge responsibilities which will build self-esteem.

Many parents who want to see samples of their child's work may ask to see the work of other children, so they may understand the standards their own child should be able to attain. If such work is displayed, it should not be identified, and a comparison should not be made between one child's achievement and that of another. The kindergarten teacher can explain what her goals are for their particular child, in relationship to his ability. She could say, "I am sure that your Tommy is very capable of doing something like this. He should be encouraged to give any task his best effort. He has ability, and we must help him to believe in himself."

The parents then understand that the teacher has not set up arbitrary standards of achievement, but is suggesting that Tommy should be guided to the best work of which he is capable.

Occasionally a conference with a parent can be quite difficult if the parent has a long-harbored antagonism toward all teachers, which is a childish carry-over from his own youth. The kindergarten teacher can quickly disarm such a parent by allowing him to express all his pent-up resentment at the beginning of the interview; thus her sympathetic attention and understanding helps the parent to freely express his opinions and discuss his problems. She can then quietly remind him that she needs his confidence if she is to help his child. When he feels that he is a *partner* in planning for his child, he is more willing to approve the teacher's use of new, unfamiliar methods which he may not understand but which she assures him will be effective with his child.

There are some other surprising and unreasonable attitudes which parents may entertain toward their child's teacher, which may require all the tact and diplomacy she can use to convince them of her sincere desire to help their child. Once convinced, such parents often become the teacher's strongest allies and friends.

Contacts with parents need not be limited to personal interviews and visits to school or home. There are a variety of opinions among educators about periodic reports to parents, or report cards for children in primary grades. Many kindergarten teachers find that report cards for their young children are too impersonal and even inaccurate. No mark on a card can show a kindergartner's delight in exploring, in experimenting, his growth in social or emotional adjustment, his enthusiasm for expressing himself in song and rhythms, in dramatizations. No mark can adequately express a child's delight in making things with his hands, the intense pride he takes in being a valued member of a group.

Contacts with parents should not be limited to discussions of problems. Warm, appreciative notes can be sent to parents now and then, showing them the teacher's gratitude for their help and expressing her pleasure in working with their children, her pride and satisfaction in their growth in learning.

Friendly, informative notes may help the parents to understand that their child's learning progress is being assessed in relationship to *his* abilities, and is not being evaluated in relationship to the progress of any other kindergartner. Such a note assures the parents that the school is offering their child the education best suited to his own developmental level. It convinces the parents that the teacher is concerned with the welfare of the whole child, his physical, mental, emotional and social well-being.

In some schools kindergarten teachers like to send home observational evaluation sheets, so parents can understand their child's progress and make a judgment for themselves in what areas he shows immaturity and the need for their help at home.

Such a list might include the following concepts:

Social living. What are your child's relationships with other children in the neighborhood? With grown-ups? Does he enjoy school, his family, excursions, picnics, trips? Is your child self-centered? Does he willingly share with family, friends? Can he recognize his own wrong-doing?

Responsibility. Can your child work independently? Does he take care of and put away materials and toys? Can he dress himself? Can he follow directions? Does he complete assigned tasks? Does he follow rules of safety which you have set up in your home?

Reading-readiness ability. Has your child a good command of words, can he tell a story, relate ideas in sequence? Does he enjoy hearing stories, does he want to look at books, pictures? Does he prefer to watch TV constantly or does he have a variety of interests? Does your child see relationships of things, likenesses and differences, big and little, in and out, up and down, etc.? Does he hear well, see well? Does he recognize colors? Can he count objects, and relate number experiences to everyday living?

Activities. Does your child enjoy working with crayons, paints, clay, or scissors? Does he enjoy listening to music? Does he sing songs learned at school? Is he interested in nature? Does he ask questions about nature? Is he curious about how mechanical things work? Is he interested in games and sports? Does he enjoy the outdoors? Does he avoid physical activity?

The parents may have suggestions about other phases of their child's development not listed here, so the teacher may need to explain the objectives in her overall planning for kindergartners. This is a reiteration of what she has said at parent-teacher meetings or private interviews, but is often necessary so there may be an exchange of constructive ideas between parents and teacher.

Teacher's Observation of Child Makes Conference Necessary

The kindergarten teacher watches a child every day in the close confines of her room as he plays and works with other boys and girls his own age. She is always aware of existing individual differences among children and takes them into account when she observes the behavior of a particular child. There are some areas of behavior, however, in which children should be expected to develop in somewhat the same way, so they may meet the demands of social living. Any deviation from these patterns of behavior is a matter of concern to her.

Parents are sometimes quite shocked to discover that their little daughter has very poor vision and needs glasses, or that their son cannot clearly see the stairs he is trying to climb. When questioned about his stumbling into furniture the parents may reply, in surprise, "Sure, he stumbles. He's all feet. He's an awkward kid."

In one old building a kindergarten teacher was obliged to take her students up and down stairs to the restroom. Carlos stumbled on the stairs when he went with the group, and he avoided going to the restroom alone. One day, when his teacher discovered that he was quite wet, he confessed that the stairs frightened him because he couldn't tell where the steps were.

His mother came alone to the conference about Carlos. She was nervous and apologetic. Yes, she knew that Carlos stumbled against things at home, and when he did he made his father mad. She protested vigorously against having Carlos' eyes examined, because they couldn't afford to pay for an eye doctor. Fortunately his teacher could reassure her that the examination would cost nothing, so she consented to take him.

Carlos had very poor vision, and the teacher was called immediately by the boy's irate father. He demanded to talk to her.

At first the father was angry, unreasonable and unbelievably rude; but he was also deeply hurt and frightened, as the kindergarten teacher soon discovered from his conversation. He was proud of his son, and had great expectations that he would become an athlete. The kid, he said, was awkward, stumbled around, couldn't even catch a ball. He didn't know what to do with him. Illogically he accused Carlos' teacher of meddling because the eye-examination had forcibly proved to him that Carlos had very bad vision, that he might never be the athlete of his father's dreams. At this point he had no compassion for his son who was handicapped. He was overwhelmed by his own disappointment and anger at his son's imperfection.

The interview was a long and difficult one. The teacher explained that there were many things the child and his father could do together, if he were outfitted with glasses. His father could show him many new and wonderful things. They could have exciting experiences together. Carlos needed his father's understanding and help. Could he have it? Once the father admitted the existence of his boy's problem he was able to discuss it without anger. The interview ended with a friendly "we'll work together" agreement between parent and teacher, and the promise that his father would buy the glasses.

Child's Reaction to School Prompts
Grandmother to Ask for Conference

It is not uncommon for a kindergarten teacher to receive an urgent note from a parent. "My child complains of a stomach ache every day and refuses to attend school. I thought he (or she) loved school. What has happened?" Every kindergarten teacher is familiar with the many reasons why Susie or Tommy suddenly gets a stomach ache to avoid attending school, so those reasons will not be discussed here. The note about Davy was from his grandmother, who was obliged to raise her daughter's little boy. She was perturbed over what she called, in her note of complaint, "the harm kindergarten has done to my grandson. He is a changed child and I don't like it."

In the first conference about Davy his grandmother said, "Davy was always so nice and quiet, just like his mother when she was little. Since he started to school he's a regular roughneck. He yells when he plays and his friends run around in my house and they all fight. What has school done to my lovely, quiet, well-mannered grandson?"

It took her some months to become convinced that Davy was a very normal little boy who was, for the first time in his life, enjoying the rough play so dear to boys his age. His grandmother tried to understand the ways in which he differed from that little girl she had raised, but it was hard for her. She visited the kindergarten often, to assure herself that Davy's behavior was normal, that he needed vigorous play and the companionship of other little boys. She and his teacher had many conferences, but not because the *child* had problems. His grandmother seemed to need the quiet assurance of his teacher that Davy was developing in ways that were natural to a healthy, curious, intelligent boy.

Child's Strange Behavior at School and at Home Makes Conference Necessary

Norton was a child with a severe emotional problem, but his teacher was not told when he entered school. There was no mention of it in his health record, which was obtained in a pre-kindergarten check-up. His teacher was unaware that he received constant medication to keep him quiet and tranquil at school. She realized that Norton's responses were slow, and she planned to ask for a conference with his parents so she might discuss his lack of progress in the simplest learning activities.

One day Norton had a tantrum and his behavior became so erratic during the next two hours that the kindergartners were frightened and his teacher was exhausted with her efforts to calm him.

An immediate conference with his mother served to inform the teacher of Norton's long record of difficulties. It helped her to know how to handle him when his tensions built up so much he could not bear to remain in the classroom. While most children do not have Norton's serious problem, many young kindergartners do come to school filled with tensions which have built up from intolerable situations in the home. They are apt to release these tensions in aggressiveness, crying, tantrums or complete withdrawal from the group. School situations might induce the same reactions at home. In either case the parents and teacher must work together and help the child to better learning.

When the teacher enrolls a child in kindergarten she should make a note on his enrollment card about food allergies, his need for regular medication, and the like. Information about Norton's problems would have helped his teacher, and his parents regretted not having voluntarily supplied it. If such information is not on the child's health record, then the teacher should ask for it.

Examples of Problems Solved by "Talking It Out" with Parents

Three weeks after the beginning of school a kindergarten teacher received this note from a parent. "Hugh is bored with school. He isn't being challenged. May I discuss this matter with you?"

She was glad to arrange the conference, for Hugh had been a puzzle to her. He did not respond to the kindergarten program. He refused to participate in games. Hugh was obviously an unhappy, discontented little boy.

For the first part of the conference his teacher kept the conversation on a "getting to know each other" basis, for Hugh's family was new to the community. She quietly listened to his mother's remarks about Hugh's preschool years and the care and attention his family had given him.

"He had two years of nursery school before we moved here," the mother said. "We told him that he would probably get to be your most important helper in kindergarten, because he would know so much more than the children who had never been to nursery school. Now Hugh is disgusted with school because you aren't giving him special attention, and he wants to learn to read."

The aims and goals of the kindergarten program were outlined in detail. Hugh's teacher explained that she was aware of the differences in cultural background among the members in her group and that now and then children entered school completely satiated with play activities. Those children were her special concern, for their interest had to be aroused before they really enjoyed kindergarten.

"I know what he wants," his mother interrupted. "He wants to be a boss. Hugh is a natural-born boss."

His teacher agreed. Hugh was a boss, but *not* a wise leader. He made demands upon his classmates, and they resented his manner. They were beginning to reject him in their play groups. He refused to play by the rules because he always wanted his own way.

"We can both help him to a better adjustment at school," his teacher suggested. "Perhaps your older son can change Hugh's expectations that he will learn to read. You see this particular kindergarten does not teach a child to read. That experience is reserved for first grade. Kindergartners are given many learning experiences here that prompt an intense *desire* to read, however, and alert children learn to recognize many words in the room, signs on the street and labels on objects."

Many conferences were held between Hugh's mother and teacher as they helped him to become responsible for his own actions. Eventually he was ready to assume the leadership he so desperately sought. He was grouped at school with some creative children whose activities challenged his interest. Hugh's boredom disappeared, and he began to show self-control and maturity.

Bertie was a child who loved to draw, to make things with his hands. He was not skillful, but his projects seemed to delight him. He became so engrossed that he was quite oblivious to the presence of his classmates around him. The kindergarten teacher watched Bertie's work with pleasure, glad to see a child so happy.

One day she overheard some companions discussing him. "That Bertie won't take his stuff home," a little girl said. "He tears up everthing. He's messy. He throws his stuff around."

The accusation was hard to believe. Bertie always seemed so proud when he left the kindergarten room with his latest product in his hand. The teacher remarked to him, as she casually walked by the table where he worked on a picture, "Your mother must love the nice things you make, Bertie."

He looked up and his blue eyes grew blank. Then he stared out the window.

"Do you give them to your mother?"

He took a deep breath and his lower lip trembled. "She don't like school stuff," he said gruffly, got up and walked away.

Bertie's mother was a lady in her late forties, the mother of ten children. He was her youngest. "What's my kid done?" she demanded, with great good humor, at the conference with his teacher. "He's always up to something."

When she was told that Bertie, for some reason, would not take home the work he so loved doing at school, she looked bewildered for a moment, then she sat up very straight. "Say," she began, "I'll bet I know what ails him. It's the big kids. My next four older than Bertie are all boys, and smart alecks, if they are mine. They bedevil that little one all the time. I've heard the boys telling him he's just a kindergarten baby and what he does is not real school work. They shame him and laugh at what he does. He does kind of botch things up, don't he? I mean, he's not very good at making things."

She was a very understanding mother and honest about her own attitude toward Bertie's accomplishments. "The poor little guy. I'm awful busy all the time, but that's no excuse, mind you, and I'm as guilty as the boys. I've probably laughed and brushed him aside when he wanted to show me something. We'll make a change at our house, I'll promise you that! My kids really love Bertie, and they'll help when I explain how things are for him. They just got carried away by that 'big-I, little-you' stuff. We'll make Bertie so proud of what he makes he'll carry every little thing home."

Before she left Bertie's mother said warmly, "I've been to school a lot of times since my first one started kindergarten. You know, there have been some bad problems with my kids over the years, but there never was one that couldn't be straightened out when their father and I got together with the teacher and sometimes the principal, too, and talked it over."

11

How to Keep a Very Bright Kindergartner Interested and Learning Up to His Potential

In most kindergartens the children with whom a teacher works have not been tested in any way and will not be tested until they have reached first grade, or later. The kindergarten teacher must evaluate the abilities of each child she teaches, using her own observation of the child, any information she may acquire from the child's parents, and in rare cases information from nursery or pre-kindergarten records to help her in making a judgment.

The discussion of bright children in this book is concerned with kindergartners who have already developed or may develop those qualities which indicate to their teacher that they are very bright intellectually or creatively.

What is meant by the term "very bright" as it is used in this chapter and elsewhere in this book? What are those qualities which a kindergartner must possess to be considered a bright child?

For the purposes of this book the following qualities are listed as criteria which the kindergarten teacher may find helpful in making a judgment concerning children whom she believes to be creatively or intellectually bright.

A very bright child:

1. Has good powers of observation and can describe what he sees.
2. Has a large vocabulary which he uses well. Can comprehend words of others.
3. Has a long attention span and can listen or concentrate on stories or projects for a longer period than the average child.
4. May demonstrate creative ability in art, music, science or manipulative skills. May show unusual proficiency in singing, dramatizations, rhythms, drawing or other phases of art.
5. Has originality in verbal expression of thoughts.
6. Shows comprehension of spatial relationships. Is able to discover cause-and-effect relationships.
7. Can solve simple problems in unique ways. Can use past experiences in attacking new problems.
8. Can reason *why* things happen and suggest the results of some actions.
9. Can see similarities between two seemingly unrelated objects.
10. Can learn by association.
11. Has understanding of the way things fit together, can distinguish between objects that are the same in all features but length and breadth, is curious about the changing appearance of objects when viewed from different angles.
12. Has ingenuity and drive. Is enthusiastic about accepting responsibilities. Gladly accepts tasks within and even beyond his capabilities.
13. Likes to observe and evaluate what he sees; to question, explore, experiment and manipulate.
14. Has desire to excel and uses much initiative and perseverance to satisfy that desire.
15. Has good imagination and original ideas.

16. Is usually emotionally stable and mature, *but not always*. Is sometimes intellectually mature but socially immature.

The qualities a young child shows are usually the result of his native, inborn ability and the influence of his environment. Some children may have great *creative* potential, or unusual manipulative skills. Intellectually bright children are not always talented, but very talented children are apt to be intellectually superior in a general way.

Bright children may differ from one another in their ability to think abstractly, in their verbal or mathematical skills, their spatial imagination, in creative arts, music, dramatics. Very bright children are not necessarily equally superior in all areas.

A kindergarten teacher may not immediately discover a bright child's potential for several reasons. The child may be so shy, so overwhelmed by the children around him that he will not disclose his abilities and interests for many months after the beginning of school. A child may have come from a home environment that has not encouraged his creative abilities, or even been aware of them. Some homes deliberately stifle performances by their children that depart in any way from the familiar and usual. Children from culturally deprived homes, or children whose families have low socio-economic status often do not develop outstanding abilities in preschool years because of parental indifference or parental incompetence to offer any stimulation of the child's latent abilities. Some families offer little encouragement to the child who is curious about words, who loves to sing, to draw, to make things, to experiment. Young children from such homes need time and the many enriching, joyous experiences of kindergarten to stimulate them in developing the abilities which have already been mentioned; however, they may noticeably display them after having attended school for some months.

There are other qualities often found in the unusually creative child which will be discussed later in this chapter in great detail. The bright child who does creative thinking differs somewhat from the child who thinks along conventional lines in his approach to learning. The kindergarten teacher must be aware of the creative child's need to express himself in his own individual way. She will be sensitive to the goals which she must set up for those bright children who are creative thinkers; and the somewhat different goals for those bright children who think in a conventional way.

Recognition of Child's Ability by Teacher

In those early days of kindergarten, when the teacher is getting acquainted with all the members of her class, she will often observe children with outstanding qualities of leadership, alertness, sustained attention, resourcefulness, and intense curiosity. As she introduces new activities and learning situations she watches the reactions of these children, and she concludes that some of them will require additional activities to challenge their interest and their unusual abilities. They may appear to be intellectually bright or creatively superior to the average five-year-old in her room. A child's intellectual ability often shows itself in conversations, in discussions, in story telling, in his excellent abstract reasoning. His boundless enthusiasm for new experiences, the intelligent and pertinent observations he makes in class are indications that he will be able to learn more quickly than the average child.

Parent-Teacher Conferences

The parents and teacher of a child who shows unusual intelligence or creativity will want to help each other set up learning programs at school and at home that will challenge the child. When discussing a child's abilities with his parents there are some questions the teacher will want to ask to establish his cultural background. Has he traveled about the country in planned trips with his parents? Has he lived in many states when his father's work has kept the family constantly on the move? Are there older brothers and sisters at home who have given the child much helpful attention? Have they stimulated his curiosity and given him good answers to his questions? Does he enjoy and seem to comprehend the conversation of adults?

There are other questions the teacher will want to ask the parents, and their answers will serve as a guide in evaluating the child's preschool experiences. Did the child walk and talk at an early age? Did he communicate well, using words, phrases, entire sentences to express himself? Was he very curious? Observant? Did he investigate objects that interested him? Did he experiment and take things apart to see how they worked? Could he make use of information learned when new situations arose that puzzled him? Was he persistent in trying to satisfy his curiosity?

Did he show an early interest in stories and pictures? Was he attentive, could he listen to an entire story? Did he spend much time looking at books? Did he later ask to have them read to him? Was he curious about objects he saw being used by older children in the family, like atlases, maps and globes? Did he demand an explanation for the use of rulers, measures, calendars, clocks, or want their use demonstrated so simply he could comprehend it? Did he draw at an early age? Was he aware of differences in colors and did he use various colors in his drawings? Was he unusually skillful in the use of his hands? Did he respond to music, enjoy rhythms?

Was he adept at fitting small objects together, or in sequential order? Was he perceptive in detecting likenesses and differences, ins and outs, ups and downs? Was he aware of spatial relationships? Could he concentrate on an interesting project for a longer period than most young children?

Some schools have counseling facilities for testing a child who has shown evidences of unusual intellectual ability in the home, when the parents request the test. Such tests may show that a child's ability has been overestimated by his parents; others verify the parents' assessment of their child's intelligence and potential. If the child is quite young, he may have intellectual maturation which far exceeds his social maturation, and need more time to become socially ready for the interaction with other children at school.

Observation of Child's Reaction to Kindergarten

From the first moment she meets a new group of kindergartners their teacher observes each child's response to the activities she provides for the group's learning enjoyment. She watches the shy child's response, first to one other child, then to the group; the bright, confident, self-assured child's assumption of leadership; the creative child's delight at finding so many materials and objects with which to express himself. She observes the culturally deprived child progress from bewilderment and weariness of the new and unfamiliar to excitement and acceptance of the satisfying experiences which have been planned for him. The young child who has spent his preschool years in a rigidly strict home where children are "seen but not heard" responds to his teacher's assurance of love, her interest in *him* and what he does, her approval; then he can use his new-found confidence and investigate, experiment, discover.

Some of these kindergartners will develop into students whose contributions to the group convince her that here are exceptionally talented children who need specially planned programs to satisfy their desire for knowledge and enrichment. One child may show outstanding intellectual ability in all activities, while another is a creative thinker, who delights his group with his original ideas and suggestions. Discovery of exceptional ability among young children is always an exciting experience for a kindergarten teacher. Some teachers have insisted, "I've never had a really bright child in *my* room, they're all very average," but they will proudly relate the story of the child who had an intense love of rhythms and music, who could organize games better than some adults. "He became a famous basketball star and an outstanding coach." They may tell about the child who was creative, with a vivid imagination and a command of words which she could weave into stories that held her classmates' attention day after day. *She* became a published writer in her teens. They will then add, "I did have this one little boy. He loved to direct dramatizations. He could get performances out of my most hopeless students. That child knew *so much* about the way people feel and think. Do you know what he turned out to be? An evangelist! He's a crusader for religion and people flock to him wherever he goes. I knew he was going to be somebody special when he grew up!"

Child's Reaction to Other Children

Many bright kindergartners show surprising qualities of leadership and insist on being given responsibilities, which they discharge efficiently. They may assume the task of helping their shy, immature classmates adjust to school. Bright, self-assured children can be observed, at play time, with a group of children gathered around them. One child may be telling a story, another will be using a flannel board, charts or other teaching devices in the room to "teach" number skills or reading-readiness skills. Some children are ingenious in discovering new and exciting approaches to familiar learning situations and will introduce them to their classmates as a game.

Not all very bright children are gregarious, however, and the kindergarten teacher must be sensitive to those who need to be quiet and undisturbed. A little boy may be friendly enough, but prefer to work alone on some project that interests him; he may be a perfectionist and will not seek or want the help of his classmates in completing the task he has set himself. A creative little girl may be making some object from many materials and her design is intricate, her work precise and detailed; so the interference of other children is so painful to her she resists them with tears or physical blows when sufficiently aggravated. The teacher observes and respects such children who must sometimes work alone and unassisted.

Planned Program of Accelerated Activities

Just as the kindergarten teacher avoids labeling any child in the room as *superior,* she will as carefully avoid making the accelerated program, which she plans for her very bright children, an obvious one; instead she will set up new objectives for those children, plan learning experiences which will attain those objectives and offer them to any child who cares to participate.

She has talked to them about their interests, listened to them discuss their interests with other children, made her own observations about their capabilities, and she is acutely aware of her obligation to open up new horizons of knowledge for her very bright students. Her plans will use as their base any subject matter about which they are curious, or material which needs their research; experiments will be conducted and projects developed in their areas of interest. As a child acquires new knowledge he will be encouraged to share his learning experiences with his group, so all the children can enjoy his special interest. Average learners often become involved in these projects, too, and make excellent contributions, so the accelerated program benefits the entire group.

Children's questions, however puzzling or irrelevant, should be answered by their teacher in a statement of fact or by her suggestion, "Let's try together to find the answer to your question." She may then want to involve other children in the discovery; or she may feel it wiser, due to the particular nature of the question, to work with the child herself. There are many ways she may suggest which will help children to find answers to their questions. Most kindergarten children cannot read, of course, but when resource books with excellent pictures are available to them, they can acquire an amazing quantity of factual knowledge from them. In one kindergarten, where American Indians were being studied, such resource books as *The American Indian, Famous Indian Tribes, Indian Crafts and Lore, Our Indian Heritage* and many others were used. (See Bibliography in the back of this book for authors and other titles.)

This resource was used when the children made Indian masks and shields. The simple tools used by early American Indians were discussed. Designs of Indian bead work and weaving proved of great interest and the children made a few simple craft objects of their own, using similar simple tools and materials.

With this background knowledge of early American Indian culture the children were eager to learn about our modern, twentieth-century Indians. Many stories were read to them and they consulted their resource books, looking at the pictures and discussing them together. They contrasted the life of the modern Indian with their own and increased their vocabularies by many words. They made up simple stories of their own, using the facts they had learned. They attempted sand painting. They designed jewelry out of tinfoil, using Indian designs and decorating the jewelry with small stones or bits of colored glass. These activities gave them an idea of the Indian as a craftsman.

Such books as *Little Wolf, Running Fox, Wakapoo and the Flying Arrows, When the Moon Is New, The Indian and His Pueblo, Little Antelope, The Mighty Hunter* and *Good Hunting Little Indian* were read to the children and used as source material by them. The stories were interesting to the entire group, but the very bright children became interested in trying to make models of adobe dwellings and totem poles with authentic Indian designs on them after they had learned what some of the designs meant; they wanted to make hogans, long houses, tepees, and chikis (summer homes of the Seminoles in Florida, which some children had seen in the Everglades). (See bibliography for books.)

Another group of kindergartners became very interested in Eskimos when an Eskimo-carved, soapstone figure of hunter and seal was brought to school by a child. The resulting study, not only of the ancient ways of the Eskimos, but of the ways in which twentieth-century Eskimos have changed their ways of living, was a delightful one to every child in the room, for the children shared in the activities that accompanied their learning experiences. The very bright students brought in pictures, helped to make charts, suggested games which would teach number and reading-readiness concepts.

Other projects can be planned with every-child participation, but open up new areas of learning for alert, bright children. Some of these are space travel, transportation, wheels and simple machines, and a wide range of science experiments. Any of these will claim the interest of every child in the room; but they also serve to offer the bright child the accelerated program he needs. He will build objects, do research, bring in additional information and initiate experiments. Several children can be grouped together for such a program and the learning which results is gratifying.

Many centers of interest in a kindergarten room challenge the imaginations of children. Tables of materials encourage their creative skills and suggest experimentation. A well-planned program provides ample time for special displays of work done at school and away from school, so a child may experience the joy and satisfaction of sharing his knowledge and skills with his classmates. The teacher will take time to record original stories and songs, and encourage discussions and exchanges of opinions. Such experiences as these are necessary to the bright children who are constantly enlarging their vocabularies and finding new ways to communicate with others; but such experiences are also joyous ones for the average learner, for he is encouraged to undertake projects of his own, alone or with a group. Even very slow learners will sometimes show a desire to join a particular enrichment program, and they should be encouraged to attempt any activity which interests them. It is not unlikely that the slow learner will reach far beyond his hitherto limited capabilities. His companions often will help him to achieve some satisfying goals.

Any expanded kindergarten program for the very bright child should be a flexible one, but a planned one; it should not be merely permissive, one which lets the bright child aimlessly entertain himself or alleviate his boredom by "doing more of the same," or by doing "whatever he wants to." The program which is offered will have definite learning goals as the teacher provides an acceleration program to coincide with her regular schedule.

Responsibilities of Teacher to Challenge Child's Abilities

On the kindergarten level the very bright child is receiving his first introduction to school, so it is very important that the experience be a happy, satisfying one. Unless his interest is constantly challenged he may become bored, or develop a behavior problem. Occasionally a bright child, whose curiosity and creativeness has been rebuffed or stifled at school, develops a feeling of guilt about his own ideas. If they are unacceptable and undesirable, are they wrong? Should he keep his thoughts to himself, and thus give his teacher the assurance that he is learning only what she expects of the other children in his class? When his school or his home continues to discourage his original thinking, his inventiveness, his intense desire to learn as much as he can about everything that interests him, the intelligent child may feel that nothing he values is worthwhile and become an underachiever. The attitude of his kindergarten teacher, then, is extremely vital to establish a love for and a satisfaction in learning which will continue to grow throughout his life.

The task of the kindergarten teacher in sustaining a planned, meaningful, richly rewarding program for children on every level of learning is not always an easy one. She may be so overwhelmed by large numbers of young children, in overcrowded, poorly equipped classrooms that she actually feels she has no time or energy to plan an accelerated program for a few very bright children. Some teachers have children with severe behavior problems or have their teaching schedules constantly interrupted by the problems of mentally or physically handicapped students. They must resort to setting up centers of interest, providing what materials are available for creative work and experimentation and allow the quick-thinking kindergartners to devise ways of acquiring additional knowledge on their own initiative.

These additional experiences can supplement the teacher's planned program: films, film strips, trips and excursions, participation in experiments and demonstrations. Some teachers seek outside help from their community to augment their program. A parent may come to talk or demonstrate some machine or learning device. Persons from foreign countries who talk about children of other lands can contribute real pleasure and learning to a group of kindergartners. Special teachers in a school system who are not scheduled for regular visits to kindergartens may offer help and suggestions in individual cases. Often a kindergarten teacher may want to enlist the help of a child's parents in continuing or assisting with a child's enrichment program in the home.

Child's Creativity Encouraged

There are many kinds of creativeness to be considered in this discussion. Some children are creative in art, music and the sciences, with unusual manipulative skills. There are other children who are intellectually creative, whose thinking diverges from the usual. There are children with a problem-solving creativity who can use existing facts to produce new ideas or arrive at new solutions. There are children who have what is sometimes called affective creativity, which manifests itself in the skills a child possesses, in his interests, in his personality, in the success he can achieve when he attempts a project. This creativity is usually expressed in story telling, dramatizations, music and various forms of art-expression.

A creative child's potential manifests itself in a number of ways. He may:

1. Be curious about objects, answers, ideas. (*How* do things work? Why? When? Where? *How much?* What is inside?)
2. Show ingenuity. (If a thing doesn't work in one way, try another. In how many ways can one object function?)
3. Have a questioning attitude. (Is the answer you gave me *always* right? If it is always true, could other answers also be true, for the same thing?)
4. Have a distinct awareness of his own needs and the overwhelming desire to experiment, investigate, manipulate and acquire new knowledge until those needs are met.
5. Have an intense need for the opportunity to work on individual projects, together with sufficient time to complete them.
6. Have original ideas about art procedures, colors, stories, events, objects.

Not all creative children have all the qualities above. The kindergarten teacher will discover their creative abilities from the things they say and do, their approach to any activity or task. She may find that some children who persist in using their own creative ideas and refuse to conform in any way to the accepted ideas of their group can be disruptive in the classroom. A teacher may be so annoyed by such a child that she will label him a "troublemaker," but the very creativeness which makes him rebel against explicit directions will, if she can be patient and direct it into constructive channels, make him a valued, contributing member of the group.

Children who do creative thinking can often find the solution to a problem in a quicker, easier way than that which is accepted by the group. The constant questions of the creatively bright young child can become annoying to his parents and teacher when adults consider his "Yes, but . . ." as impudent, rebellious and uncooperative, and a manifestation of his unwillingness to accept the opinions of others.

The kindergarten teacher will encourage a child's creative thinking, lest he feel guilty because he cannot accept explanations without questioning them. He needs assurance that wanting to know *more* about a subject is commendable and that his teacher will help him to find out what he wants to know. She will have patience with his inability to conform, and appreciate the spontaneity of his questions and contributions, and use them, when possible, to spark the interest of her entire group.

Creative children sometimes attempt a project that is beyond their physical power to complete, or try to make something for which they do not have the correct tools or materials. When a child becomes frustrated and discouraged his teacher's suggestion, "Let's look at this together and talk about it. Perhaps you can do this another way," or "Perhaps you can figure out a *new* way . . ." is a welcome one.

Most kindergarten teachers find that the reactions of creative thinkers are delightful, for they usually have an excellent sense of humor and their remarks are unexpected, sometimes even disrupting! When most kindergartners interpret a story they have heard, they make simple pictures of familiar objects and often depend on each other for ideas. A creative child tells a story *his* way, draws an object the way *he* sees it but certainly not always the way his startled teacher expects him to see it.

If she asks, "What is a house?" the average or intellectually bright child might answer, "A house is a place to live" or "A house is a building where I live" or "A house is made of many things, wood, stones, sometimes blocks of snow." The creative thinker might answer, "A house keeps you cosy and warm and I would like to try every kind of house there is, in holes in trees and in a turtle's shell, but I might think it's too dark to live under the ground in a snake's house."

In a discussion about the numeral five a creative child might begin to chant, "I've got a five. I've got a beehive. Five beehives. How many bees can fly in a beehive?" and somebody may suggest, "More'n five!" About that time the teacher may have to adroitly quiet the confusion.

When a creative thinker contributes more than one answer to a question, interesting discussion often results. This allows participation by his class. If asked to name the color of a yellow object he might answer, "That's the color of a lemon and the moon when it's like a teeny-tiny cutoff fingernail. A moon fingernail! You should see how yellow our baby's chin looks underneath when I hold a dandelion under it. He likes butter. I like butter better'n oleo, but my Mom says we can't afford butter. I guess my baby better like oleo if he wants to eat at our house."

Conventional thinkers and creative thinkers sometimes react quite differently to familiar objects. If given a box filled with brightly colored paper shapes of triangles, rectangles, squares and circles, the conventional thinker will make conventional objects from the shapes. He will make wagons, trucks, candlesticks, or abstract designs. The creative thinker may come up with an intricate picture and a story to go with it. "See these triangle babies? They have round heads because their mama has a round head. This one has a square head and a round body. He's different because he wants to do things the other babies can't do. When he falls down he rolls. When they fall down they bump all over the place. This one's sharp stomach sticked right into him when he fell over."

The creativity of all children, whether very bright or average learners, can be encouraged and developed. The child whose creativity is unusual is a child who finds joy and satisfaction in *many* activities. As he grows older the results of his work are often outstanding.

Child's Valuable Contribution to Group

Children who have those qualities and characteristics which indicate that they are very bright, either intellectually or creatively, can be a real asset in the kindergarten room. Teachers should encourage them to assume responsibilities, become leaders, share their abilities with their classmates. One kindergartner who played the piano very well enjoyed playing for group singing. She and a group of other kindergartners who particularly enjoyed music composed some original songs and their teacher wrote them down. One little boy who read fluently when he entered kindergarten volunteered to pass out folders, to read stories, to help his classmates find the names of states on maps and on the globe. He organized "classes" during free activity time and played a "names of things" game with his friends, using felt letters and a flannel board.

Children who have an excellent ear for sounds often will be overheard playing games with other children, using beginning sounds in their names, or they may play games of rhyming words.

Very bright children usually seek an outlet for their abundance of knowledge and are generous in sharing what they know with their classmates. The average kindergarten child casually accepts the fact that his friend "knows a lot" and he as casually shares, when he can, in his friend's activities. Participation in the accelerated program which the teacher has planned for her bright students is often a pleasant learning experience in which the average child is also involved. He absorbs all the information he can, while the very bright child continues to be challenged, interested and learning up to his potential.

12

Teaching

in a

Happy Classroom

The joyous anticipation a child feels when he enters the kindergarten room each day tends to establish a pattern for the attitude he will have toward school in the years which follow. Long after he has forgotten the routine activities of kindergarten, a child may recall small incidents that impressed him; his teacher's warmth and gaiety; her instant response to any child's need. He remembers the pleasant feeling he had each day that something interesting and exciting would happen; the pride he felt when he could contribute to an activity and be warmly praised by the teacher for his efforts.

A teacher's guidance and instruction have more far-reaching effects than she may realize and the atmosphere in her room is a long-remembered one.

Teacher Acceptance of All Children

One day, just before Christmas, a little girl and her aunt walked through a toy store together. The woman directed the

child's attention to objects of interest. "Look, Betty, isn't that
pretty? Over here are some good puzzles. Would you like a puzzle for Christmas?" The child was fretful and surprisingly unin-
terested in the colorful displays in the store. She tugged at her
aunt's arm. "Let's go home," she urged.

Suddenly the woman squatted down beside the child, until
her eyes were on a level with those of the little girl. After a
moment's quiet observation she gathered the child high in her
arms and stood erect. "No wonder you whined, Betty," she said.
"If all *I* could see in a store were knees and wooden counters
I'd whine, too! I might even *yell!*" She continued to carry the
child in her arms and they enjoyed the displays together, for
now they could see the same objects; they could put their own
evaluation on the experiences they were sharing.

No teacher can give warm acceptance and understanding to
all the children in her room until she has learned to look at each
child's world through his eyes. She may find, with a neglected
or culturally deprived child, that she must continue to help him
at *his* level until she can understand all the experiences he has
had there. Then she may find ways to help him to a level where
he may meet and enjoy the new and exciting world of learning
which she will provide for him.

Children of all ages learn best when the schoolroom atmosphere is a relaxed one of pleasant, shared experiences; when their
teachers are understanding, good-natured, loving and receptive
to their interests and individual requirements.

A good teacher must have the inner strength to subordinate
her own desires and inclinations to the needs of the child, if she
is to have his complete confidence. She must be aware of all
the ways she can help him to a maximum of learning without
pressure or conflict. Her frequent laughter and gay approach
to his problems can make the learning experience a joyous one
for a child. Her calm, even-tempered acceptance of unpleasant
situations can give her a dignity and stability that is warmly
comforting to the child who has known little of acceptance and
security. He soon understands that she is one person who will
love him when his behavior is undesirable; that his efforts to
improve will be rewarded by her encouragement and praise. He

may find rejection and dislike elsewhere in his life, but in his own schoolroom he is somebody special to his teacher.

Giving of herself helps a teacher to make kindergartners feel her warmth and acceptance. She asks them to share their interests and their needs with her, but she in turn shares many of *her* interests with them. She laughs with them, she sometimes teases gently, she shows genuine enjoyment in a child's comments or favorite possessions. She likes being teased a little by her students, but always maintains that delicate balance of good taste in any teacher-pupil relationship.

Self-discipline with Teacher-guidance
Is Key to Happy Room

Every kindergarten teacher knows the value of self-discipline for five-to-six-year-olds. Helping her young students to acquire self-discipline is one of the kindergarten teacher's chief objectives. Her plans for them, her personal attitudes of warm, loving acceptance and genuine interest in them, and the atmosphere which she establishes in her room help young children to assume responsiblity for their own conduct. She sets a pattern for their attitudes and behavior toward each other. They observe their teacher's kindness and they glow when she appreciates their efforts. In an atmosphere of such respect for each individual child, they, too, find it easy to be tolerant. They will praise their classmates' achievements. They accept those children whose mannerisms are often annoying and hard for them to understand. Their teacher is consistent in her attitude that each child in the room is equally loved and valued, and firm in her disapproval of misbehavior which disrupts the learning activities and pleasures of the group. Children soon understand that they may work and play independently or in groups, making their own decisions and being responsible for their own behavior so long as another child's rights and pleasures are not being threatened.

In the room where self-discipline is encouraged by the teacher, children learn that a mistake can be made without the need to feel guilt or fear. Groups of children learn to work and play together with tolerance for differences of opinion, because the whole atmosphere in the room is one of genuine belief in the ability of young children to be responsible for their own behavior.

Being a good friend to others so they, in turn, will be friendly, and looking for and praising the nice qualities of the children are attitudes which kindergartners observe in their teacher and emulate as they strive for self-discipline.

The teacher tempers her rejection of unacceptable behavior with the warm assurance of her love; and never lets any child leave the classroom with a feeling that his misconduct is unforgiven. The young child observes her understanding and re-evaluates any previously acquired ideas he may have had about "an eye for an eye," or "you do something to me, I'll do ten times worse to you." He discovers that his conceptions of revenge are not acceptable in the happy kindergarten room. He makes great progress toward self-discipline when he begins to view his own behavior objectively and makes a determination to be "one of the good guys."

Excellent Planning and Organization of Learning Situations Vital

Not every kindergarten teacher can be fortunate enough to teach in a modern, well-lighted, well-equipped room; but every teacher can have an attractive room to which her students come every day with joy and anticipation. She can be ingenious in using what equipment and materials she has and set up attractive centers of interest. The warmth of her personality, her friendliness and smiling response to her students can make even the shabbiest, most inadequately equipped room seem beautiful; one to which they will come each day with pleasure and leave each day with reluctance.

The physical appointments in the kindergarten room should be as attractive as possible, of course, but the stimulating atmosphere of excitement in learning, with which a good teacher surrounds her children, is far more important than materials or elaborate equipment. When acquiring new knowledge is an enjoyable adventure and each new learning activity an eagerly accepted challenge, the room is a happy one. There a child's creativeness is encouraged and his contributions valued. Provisions have been made in his teacher's plans to fully develop each child's learning potentials in relation to his age and need, to challenge his drive to learn.

The program she provides is planned so that children can work happily and creatively together in a democratic atmosphere of respect for the rights of others and appreciation for contributions they make to shared activities.

Challenging Work with Specific Learning Goals, Geared to Individual Differences

The teacher in the happy kindergarten of today continues to offer the young child time to play, to create, to experiment, to investigate, to dream as his needs and interests prompt. She allows him time to share the results of his creative work and play with his classmates, and provides him with her approval for whatever contribution he has made. She respects children as individuals whose needs differ widely. She is sensitive to the need to change her plans to accommodate the specific learning needs of one child or a group of children.

Providing for individual differences does not necessarily mean that the kindergarten teacher must do individualized teaching. Young children need to work together, to value each other's opinions and to respect the contributions of others. Kindergartners enjoy being part of a group, and derive a feeling of security in shared activities. If she must give individual help to one or more members of the group, the teacher does it unobtrusively, with respect for the child's pride.

She allows each child to respond to the learning program she provides in terms of his own ability, in ways which reflect his own readiness to accept new ideas and experiences. All activities are planned to include the interests and needs of each child in her room, so each can feel a sense of achievement, whatever his ability. The teacher helps the creative child to direct his interests into activities which will be deeply satisfying. She provides opportunities for the more advanced child in her group to experiment, investigate and learn all he can about the things which intrigue his interest.

The kindergarten teacher carefully plans a program flexible enough to offer specific learning goals to the children whose individual differences and needs vary from those of the average group. She makes sure that each child has a feeling of her genuine acceptance of him and of her pride in his individual achievements. Her smiles, her comforting response to his uncertainties convince him that he is loved, appreciated and needed. His school is indeed a happy place.

Every kindergarten teacher must set up her own program, according to the requirements of her group of children, and the policies of her school. Her program should be flexible enough, however, to provide her with time to help her kindergartners develop their interests. One young teacher wailed to another, "I *can't* squeeze everything on my schedule into a morning! I *never* catch up! There's always so much my children want to *do* and so much they want to *talk about!* How can a teacher do everything on her schedule *every day?*"

The answer is—she can't. She shouldn't even try. What a wonderful group of kindergartners that teacher must have had, with so much they wanted to do and talk about.

A kindergarten teacher's plans should include procedures which never vary from day to day. A certain amount of routine must be adhered to, because young children find security in knowing that "we do this every day." They need to know what is expected of them when they first come into their room at the beginning of school, what they may or may not look at, play with, and so on. They want procedures established for distributing milk, for dismissals, for behavior in the halls. They like a routine for putting toys away, for rest time and for activities at their tables.

The program for stories, dramatizations, music, art, physical games and "Games-that-Teach" may be widely varied each day. In this way all activities can be intensely interesting to each child, whatever his learning potential, for his teacher can adjust the schedule so that she can give individual help and encouragement when and where it is needed. The following program is only a suggested one, showing a variety of activities which can be included in a kindergarten schedule. The time allotment covers a period of two and one-half hours.

Ten Minutes.

School begins. Children immediately find quiet activities upon entering the room. They may look at books, work puzzles, check on leaders for the day, draw pictures, care for plants or pets in the room, work together in quiet groups, look at room displays, etc.

Fifteen Minutes.

Take attendance, designate leaders, check weather charts (and other charts, if any), have flag salute, show and tell (one or more days a week).

While taking attendance, children count and attendance is put up with large numerals on bulletin board or chalk board. Figures suggest many number experiences: *How many* boys are present? *How many* girls? Which group has the greatest number present? The least number? If attendance is one hundred percent, stars or other symbols may be put up beside numerals. (Many other number experiences will be suggested from these numerals, from time to time.)

Twenty Minutes.

Song-activity time. This is a time for teaching new songs and singing old favorites. Some songs lend themselves to games with physical participation, or counting experiences. There is ample time for all song activities.

Songs which are especially good to use with particular units-of-children's-interests can be introduced at this time. Seasonal songs and fingerplays of all kinds are enjoyed.

Thirty Minutes.

Planning time. This is the time when the kindergarten teacher and children plan their activities together. It is a time for stories and dramatizations, for role-playing activities, for art and construction activities.

Fifteen Minutes.	*Time for games.* Reading-readiness games, number games, games that teach skills and develop sensory perceptions may be played at this time. (Of course, such games may fit into other activities, too.)
Ten Minutes.	*Milk time.*
Fifteen Minutes.	*Free choice* of activities in the room or outdoor play.
Ten Minutes.	*Rest on rugs.*
Twenty Minutes.	*Gathering up the loose ends.* An unassigned time. Can be used for showing film strips or to play special records. A good time for teacher and children to do those things for which there was no time during the day. Children may want to work on individual projects, finish some task or set up materials for a project the next day.
	This is a time when the teacher can evaluate the day's activities. If the group has been unusually stimulated, now is the time for quiet fun, a story or a quiet game. One day a week it could be a time for the children to choose a special activity which they love, or choose stories, songs or poems which are favorites. This time should be a happy time together, a *"Today has been a wonderful day. What do you suppose will happen tomorrow?"* time.
Five Minutes.	Put on coats, boots, etc.
	Dismissal.

Behavioral Problems Reduced to a Minimum

In the atmosphere of a happy kindergarten room, where the achievements and contributions of each individual child are valued by the teacher, behavioral problems are at a minimum.

From the beginning of school their teacher has offered the kindergartners her whole-hearted acceptance, whatever their capabilities. When directions are necessary they are positive ones which the children can understand. Each child is made aware of the school rules of courtesy and safety. Their teacher helps the students to understand the reasons for those limitations she must put upon their activities. Freedom of movement is permitted in the room when the children respect the rules of good behavior.

Visitors in the happy kindergarten room are sometimes amazed that young children can continue their activities undisturbed, without making constant demands on their teacher's attention. When they are secure in the knowledge and understanding that rules of good behavior are necessary for the happiness of the whole group, they take pride in obeying rules. Their teacher can leave the room at any time and know that her students are quiet, busy and well-behaved. They have been given love and understanding, the joy of belonging to a group, praise for their achievements, and acceptance from their teacher and their companions. In such a room kindergartners love and respect their teacher. She proves her respect for them and trust in them by giving them the opportunity for independent thought and action.

A good teacher in a happy kindergarten room is one who shapes the clay of a child with love and understanding; smooths its irregularities with tender wisdom; adds touches to challenge curiosity and motivation for learning; glazes it with skills adapted to its individual needs; and fires it with the desire for knowledge until it is a complete and lovely product ready for citizenship—and *first grade*.

BIBLIOGRAPHY

Anderson, Harold H., and Helen M. Brewer, *Studies of Teachers' Classroom Personalities, I, Dominative and Socially Integrative Behavior of Kindergarten Teachers*. Applied Psychology Monographs, No. 6, 1945.

Barlowe, Sy., *Insects*. New York: Maxton Publishers, Inc., 1952.

Beatty, Hetty Burlingame, *Little Owl Indian*. Eau Claire, Wis.: E. M. Hale and Company, 1964.

Beim, Lorraine and Jerrold, *The Little Igloo*. New York: Harcourt, Brace and Company, 1941.

Berkley, Ethel S., *The Size of It*. New York: William R. Scott, Inc., 1950.

Bernard, Harold Wright, *Mental Hygiene for Classroom Teachers*. First edition; New York: McGraw-Hill, Inc., 1952.

Bonsall, Marcella Ryser, *Who Are the Gifted?* California Elementary School Administrator's Association, 1954 Year Book.

Bramley, Franklyn M., *Snow Is Falling*. New York: Thomas Y. Crowell Co., 1963.

Brewster, Benjamin, *The First Book of Indians*. New York: Franklin Watts, Inc., 1950.

Bridges, Wm., *Animal Adventures*. Racine, Wis.: Whitman Publishing Co., 1963.

Brogan, Peggy, and Lorene K. Fox, *Helping Children Learn*. Yonkers-on-Hudson, N.Y.: World Book Company, 1955.

Brumbaugh, Florence N., and Bernard Roshco, *Your Gifted Child*. New York: Henry Holt and Company, 1959.

Burch, Robert, *A Funny Place to Live*. New York: The Viking Press, Inc., 1962.

Bush, Robert, *The Teacher-Pupil Relationship*. Englewood Cliffs, N.J.: Prentice-Hall, Inc., 1954.

Carr, Marion B., *Sea and Shore*. New York: Golden Press, Inc., 1959.

Carroll, Herbert Allen, *Mental Hygiene*. Englewood Cliffs, N.J.: Prentice-Hall, Inc., 1956.

Cincinnati Public Schools, *Challenging the Able Learner*. Primary Grades, Curriculum Bulletin 301, 1957.

Copeland, Donalda, *Little Eskimos*. Chicago: Childrens Press, 1965.

Craig, Gerald, *Science for the Elementary School Teacher*. Boston: Ginn and Company, 1957.

Cruickshank, William, and G. O. Johnson, *The Education of Exceptional Children and Youth*. Englewood Cliffs, N.J.: Prentice-Hall, Inc., 1958.

Cutts, Norma Estelle, *Practical School Discipline and Mental Hygiene*. New York: Houghton Mifflin Co., 1944.

Cutts, Norma E., and Nicholas Moseley, *Providing for Individual Differences in the Elementary School*. Englewood Cliffs, N.J.: Prentice-Hall, Inc., 1960.

————, *Providing for the Bright Child in a Heterogeneous Group*. Educational Administration and Supervision 39: 225–30, April, 1953.

————, *Teaching the Bright and Gifted*. New York: Prentice-Hall, Inc., 1957.

D'Amato, Janet and Alex, *Who Goes There?* New York: Wonder Books, Inc., 1961.

De Haan, Robert, and Robert J. Havighurst, *Educating Gifted Children*. Chicago: University of Chicago Press, 1962.

De Haan, Robert F., and Jack Kough, *Helping Children with Special Needs*. University of Chicago Science Research Association, Inc., 1956.

Deming, Therese O., and Thelma Shaw, *Little Eagle*. Chicago: Albert Whitman and Company, 1958.

————, *The Indians in Winter Camp*. Chicago: Albert Whitman and Company, 1958.

de Regniers, Beatrice Schenk, *The Giant Story*. New York: Harper and Bros., Publishers, 1953.

Derman, Sarah, *The Snowman Who Wanted to Stay*. Racine, Wis.: Whitman Publishing Company, 1948.

D'Evelyn, Katherine E., *Individual Parent-Teacher Conferences*. New York: Bureau of Publications, Teachers College, Columbia University, 1945.

Dines, Glen, *Indian Pony*. New York: The Macmillan Company, 1963.

Driscoll, Gertrude, *How to Study the Behavior of Children*. New York: Bureau of Publications, Teachers College, Columbia University, 1941.

Eisner, Elliot W., "Think with Me About Creativity," *Instructor*, New York: F. A. Owen Publishing Company, December, 1962.

Epstein, Sam and Beryl, *Sea Shells*. Champaign, Ill.: Garrard Publishing Company, 1963.

Eskimo Family. New York: Encyclopaedia Britannica, Inc., 1962.

Farquhar, Margaret C., *Indian Children of America*. New York: Holt, Rinehart and Winston, Inc., 1964.

Featherstone, W. B., *Teaching the Slow Learner*. New York: Bureau of Publications, Teachers College, Columbia University, 1951.

Fletcher, Sydney E., *The American Indian*. New York: Grosset and Dunlap, Inc., 1954.

————, *The Big Book of Indians*. New York: Grosset and Dunlap, Inc., 1950.

Friskey, Margaret, *Indian Two Feet and His Eagle Feather*. Chicago: Childrens Press, 1967.

————, *Indian Two Feet and His Horse*. Chicago: Childrens Press, 1959.

Gay, Zhenya, *Who Is It?* New York: The Viking Press, Inc., 1957.

Gesell, Arnold, and Frances L. Ilg, *The Child from Five to Ten*. New York: Harper and Bros., Publishers, 1946.

Gomberg, Robert M., "Tomorrow's Family," *Child Study,* Vol. XXXIV, No. 3 (Summer 1957).

Goudey, Alice E., *Houses of the Sea.* New York: Charles Scribner's Sons, 1959.

Hader, Berta and Elmer, *The Big Snow.* New York: The Macmillan Co., 1948.

————, *Little Antelope.* New York: The Macmillan Co., 1962.

————, *Snow in the City.* New York: The Macmillan Co., 1963.

Harrington, Lyn, *Ootook, Young Eskimo Girl.* Eau Claire, Wis.: E. M. Hale and Company, 1964.

Helping Parents Understand the Exceptional Child. Proceedings of the Annual Spring Conference on Education and the Exceptional Child. Langhorne, Penn.: Child Research Clinic of the Woods School, May, 1952.

Hengesbaugh, Jane, *I Live in So Many Places.* Chicago: Childrens Press, 1956.

Hogner, Dorothy Childs, *Butterflies.* New York: Thomas Y. Crowell Company, 1962.

Holling, Holling C., *The Book of Indians.* New York: The Platt and Munk Co., Inc., 1935.

Holsaert, Eunice, *Life in the Arctic.* New York: Harvey House Publishers, 1957.

Hutchinson, William M., *Sea Shells.* New York: Maxton Publishers, Inc., 1954.

Hylander, Clarence J., *Sea and Shore.* New York: The Macmillan Company, 1950.

Hymes, James L., Jr., *Behavior and Misbehavior.* Englewood Cliffs, N.J.: Prentice-Hall, Inc., 1955.

————, *Effective Home-School Relationships.* Englewood Cliffs, N.J.: Prentice-Hall, Inc., 1953.

Jenkins, Gladys Gardner, *Helping Children Reach Their Potential.* Chicago: Scott Foresman and Company, 1961.

Jersild, A. T., *In Search of Self.* New York: Bureau of Publications, Teachers College, Columbia University, 1952.

Kay, Dorothea, *Fishes*. New York: Maxton Publishers, Inc., 1953.

Keats, Ezra Jack, *The Snowy Day*. New York: The Viking Press, Inc., 1962.

Klein, David B., *Mental Hygiene*. New York: Henry Holt and Company, 1944.

Lambert, Hazel M., *Teaching the Kindergarten Child*. New York: Harcourt, Brace and Company, Inc., 1958.

Langdon, Grace, and Irving W. Stout, *Teacher-Parent Interviews*. Englewood Cliffs, N.J.: Prentice-Hall, Inc., 1954.

Les Tina, Dorothy, *A Book to Begin on Alaska*. New York: Holt, Rinehart and Winston, Inc., 1962.

Low, Donald F., *Sea Shells*. New York: Wonder Books, Inc., 1961.

Lowenfeld, Viktor, and W. Lambert Brittain, *Creative and Mental Growth*. New York: The Macmillan Company, 1964.

McKie, Foy, and P. D. Eastman, *Snow*. New York: Random House, 1962.

Martin, Richard A., *Butterflies and Moths*. New York: Golden Press, Inc., 1958.

Martin, Teri, *The True Book of Indians*. Chicago: Childrens Press, 1954.

Moon, Grace and Carl, *One Little Indian*. Chicago: Albert Whitman and Co., 1957.

Nurturing Individual Potential. Papers and Reports from the ASCD Seventh Curriculum Research Institute, Washington, D.C.: Association for Supervision and Curriculum Development, N.E.A., 1964.

Parish, Peggy, *Good Hunting Little Indian*. New York: Young Scott Books, 1958.

Pistorious, Anna, *What Butterfly Is It?* New York: Follett Publishing Company, 1949.

Prescott, Daniel A., *Helping Teachers Understand Children*. Washington, D.C.: American Council on Education, 1945.

Radcliffe, James T., *Polar Regions*. New York: Hart Publishing Company, Inc., 1962.

Redl, F., and D. Wineman, *Children Who Hate*. Illinois: The Free Press, 1951.

Reed, Fritz, and William W. Wattenberg, *Mental Hygiene in Teaching*. New York: Harcourt, Brace and Company, Inc., 1951.

Rockwell, Anne and Harlow, *Sally's Caterpillar*. New York: Parents' Magazine Press, 1966.

Russell, Solveig Paulson, *Indian Big and Indian Little*. New York: Bobbs-Merrill Company, Inc., 1964.

Shannon, Terry, *A Dog Team for Ongluk*. Chicago: Melmont Publishers, Inc., 1962.

————, *Kidlik's Kayak*. Chicago: Albert Whitman and Company, 1959.

————, *Tyee's Totem Pole*. Chicago: Albert Whitman and Company, 1955.

————, *Where Animals Live*. Chicago: Albert Whitman and Company, 1958.

Shapp, Martha and Charles, *Let's Find Out About Animal Homes*. New York: Franklin Watts, Inc., 1962.

————, *Let's Find Out What the Signs Say*. New York: Franklin Watts, Inc., 1959.

Sheviakov, George V., and Fritz Redl, *Discipline for Today's Children and Youth*. New Rev.; Washington, D.C.: Association for Supervision and Curriculum Development, N.E.A., 1956.

Sioux Buffalo Hunters. New York: Encyclopaedia Britannica, Inc., 1962.

Swain, Su Zan N., *Insects in Their World*. New York: Garden City Books, 1955.

Symonds, Percival M., "Personality of the Teacher," *Journal of Education Research*, XL (May, 1947), pp. 652–71.

Thorman, George, *Toward Mental Health*. Public Affairs Pamphlet #120.

Torgerson, Theodore L., *Studying Children: Diagnostic and Remedial Procedures in Teaching*. New York: The Dryden Press, 1949.

Torrance, E. Paul, "Continuity in the Creative Development of Young Children," Institute for the Exploration of Early Childhood Education, Wheelock College, Boston, Nov. 6, 1964.

Tresselt, Alvin, *White Snow Bright Snow*. New York: Lothrop, Lee and Shepard Company, Inc., 1947.

True, Barbara, and Marguerite Henry, *Their First Igloo*. Chicago: Albert Whitman and Company, 1943.

Vinson, Pauline, *Willie Goes to the Seashore*. New York: The Macmillan Company, 1954.

Wackerbarth, Marjorie, *Bobby Learns About Butterflies*. Minneapolis, Minn.: T. S. Denison and Company, Inc., 1964.

Ward, Muriel, *Young Minds Need Something to Grow On*. Evanston, Illinois: Row Peterson and Company, 1957.

Webber, Irma E., *It Looks Like This*. New York: William R. Scott, Inc., 1949.

Wills, Clarice, and Lucille Lindborg, *Kindergarten for Today's Children*. Chicago: Follett Publishing Company, 1967.

Wills, Clarice, and William H. Stegeman, *Living in the Kindergarten*. Chicago: Follett Publishing Company, 1956.

Witmer, Helen L., and Ruth Kotinsky, *Personality in the Making*. New York: Harper and Bros., Publishers, 1952.

Witty, Paul, "Who Are the Gifted?" *Education for the Gifted* (Fifty-seventh Yearbook of the National Society for the Study of Education), Part II, Chicago National Society for the Study of Education, 1958.

Zachry, Caroline B., *Emotion and Conduct in Adolescence*. New York: D. Appleton Century Company, Inc., 1940.

TEACHING AIDS

FILM STRIPS

The *True* Series:

True Book of Plants.
True Book of Trees.
True Book of Insects.
True Book of Animal Homes.
True Book of Animals of Sea and Shore.

Seasons.

Spring Is Here.
Winter Is Here.
Autumn Is Here.
Summer Is Here.

Transportation.

Trucks Work for Us.
Working on the Railroad.
Railroads and Relaxation.
Round and Round Go the Wheels.
Transportation in the Past.
Water Transportation.
Highway Transportation.
Railway Transportation.
Air Transportation.
Travel in Space.

Nature

Butterflies and Moths.
Butterflies Grow.
The Caterpillar's Journey.
Animals Also Travel.
Animal Homes.
Animals That Help People Travel.
Plants and Seeds Travel.
Finding Out About Land, Air and Water.

Indians.

American Indian Unit, 10 film strips.
Where Did the Indians Live?
Eastern Forest Indians.
Pueblo Indians of the Southwest.
Indians of the Western Plains.
Indians of the Pacific Coast.
Our Indian Neighbors Today.
Learning About Indian Costumes.
Learning About Indian Houses.
Learning About Indian Dances.
Learning About Indian Crafts.
The Boyhood of Lone Raven.
The Young Manhood of Quick Otter.

Navajo Children.
Flamingo Princess of the
    Natchez.

The Journey of the Flamingo
    Princess.
Eskimo Children.
Eskimo Family.

Animal Families and Their Homes.

Mrs. Cottontail and Her Springtime Family.
Mrs. Squirrel and Her Family.
Mr. and Mrs. Mallard and Their Family.
Mr. and Mrs. Robin and Their Springtime Family.
Mrs. Bear and Her Family.
Mr. and Mrs. Beaver and Their Family.

OTHER TEACHING AIDS

ED-U-CARDS of Nature, *Sea Shells* and *Butterflies and Moths.* New York: Ed-U-Cards Manufacturing Corporation, 1961.

See-Quees (Puzzles of sequential development. *Frogs, butterflies,* etc., by JUDY.)

Index